WITHDRAWN
Introduction
to ACADEMIC WRITING

Second Edition

Alice Oshima
Ann Hogue

Longman

Introduction to Academic Writing: Second Edition

Addison Wesley Longman, 10 Bank Street, White Plains, N.Y. 10606

Editorial Director:	Joanne Dresner
Senior Acquisitions Editor:	Allen Ascher
Production Editor:	Liza Pleva
Text Design:	PC&F, Inc.
Text Adaptation:	Naomi Ganor
Cover Design:	Curt Belshe
Electronic Production Supervisor:	Kim Teixeira
Composition:	Kathleen Marks

Photo Credits: p. 1 AP/Wide World Photos; p. 2 Ron Davis/Shooting Star; p. 2 Gregg Forwerck/NBA photos; p. 24 UIF Wallin/The Image Bank; p. 31 Robert Frerck/Odyssey Productions; p. 67 David Madison; p. 69 © Allsport/Vandystadt; p. 90 Salmeron, Miguel S./FPG International Corp.; p. 92 Ford Motor Company; p. 101 Kathy Sands-Boehmer (top), Merle Sciacca (bottom); p. 105 Miami Herald photo from the American Red Cross; p. 114 James Schnepf/Gamma Liaison; p. 142 Grant Faint/The Image Bank; p. 152 James Burke/Life Magazine (top), Grant Haist (bottom); p. 167 AP/Wide World Photos; p. 190 Paul Howell/Gamma Laision (top), Robin Mayer/Gamma Laision (bottom)

Art Credits: pp. 2–3, 47, 88, 115 (top) Daisy DePuthod; pp. 13, 34, 42, 51, 63, 158, 184, 198 Mary Burkhardt; p. 115 (bottom) Mike Luckovich

Text Credit: p. 193 by Arlette Delhaxhe, Reprinted from The Christian Science Monitor and The World Media Project.

Library of Congress Cataloging-in-Publication Data

Oshima, Alice
    Introduction to academic writing / Alice Oshima, Ann Hogue.—2nd ed.
       p.   cm.
    Includes bibliographical references.
    ISBN 0-201-69509-X
      1. English language—Rhetoric—Handbooks, manuals, etc.
2. English language—Grammar—Handbooks, manuals, etc. 3. Academic writing—Handbooks, manuals, etc. I. Hogue, Ann. II. Title.
√ PE1408.072   1997
808'.042—dc20
                               96-36704
                                  CIP

16 – CRS - 070605

Dedication

To Andrew, Derek, and Ryan

Contents

Introduction

To the Teacher

Introduction to Academic Writing, second edition, is an intermediate writing textbook and workbook for nonnative speakers of English from age sixteen through adult. It is a comprehensive writing text that uses high-interest topics to teach rhetoric, grammar, and sentence structure.

This textbook contains nine units, each requiring eight to twelve hours of class time. It covers a wide range of skills, from basic punctuation and capitalization rules in Unit 1 to rather advanced clause work in Units 5, 7, 8, and 9. The organization is highly flexible, allowing teachers to select units or sections of units suitable for the varying abilities typical of intermediate classes.

The book teaches the writing process using simple, clear language that guides the students through a series of steps to produce well-organized, adequately developed paragraphs and essays. Explanations are kept simple, and numerous practices help students assimilate the points taught.

Organization of the Text

Most units have four sections: The Writing Process, Organization, Grammar and Mechanics, and Sentence Structure. A **Writing Process** section opens each unit with prewriting activities and closes it with postwriting activities. Students begin work on a topic at the beginning of each unit, ponder it while working through the unit, and perfect it at the end in a final writing assignment.

The **Organization** sections are ordered as follows. The first part of the book (Units 1 through 5) emphasizes paragraph writing. In Units 1 through 3, students work with the "easier" modes of narration and description. In Unit 4, a detailed explanation of paragraphs begins and continues in Unit 5. Unit 6 teaches basic essay organization in depth, and the remaining units expand on this information to include three essay forms: logical division (Unit 7), supporting opinions (Unit 8), and comparison-contrast (Unit 9).

The **Grammar and Mechanics** sections present items that are pertinent to the rhetorical modes being studied such as comparatives in Unit 9, or that are especially troublesome to intermediate learners of English, such as simple past vs. present perfect.

The **Sentence Structure** sections present three types of English sentences (simple, compound, and complex) in order of progressive difficulty. In the first three units, simple and compound sentences are taught and practiced extensively. Later units cover complex sentences with adverb and adjective clauses.

Changes in the Second Edition

Although the material taught in the second edition is essentially the same as in the first edition, it is presented in fresh contexts and formats. Instructors familiar with the first edition will find these differences:

- Most of the model paragraphs and essays are new, and most units now contain several models.
- The writing process has been expanded. Each unit now begins with a prewriting exercise for pair or group work, which then culminates in the final writing assignment at unit's end. This format allows the student to start thinking about the topic early on, share ideas with classmates, develop them while working through the unit, and finally distill them in the final paragraph or essay.

- The writing assignment at the end of each unit is accompanied by an *interactive editing checklist.* Each checklist covers all of the teaching points in the unit.

   Here's how students should use the editing checklists. Each list has two columns. The questions in the left column are for self-editing by the writer *before* bringing his or her first draft to class. The right column—which presents questions and interactions for evaluating a composition—should be completed in class by a peer editor. The peer editor should actually respond to each question and set of directions in the book of the student whose composition he or she is editing. The instructor might want to circulate in the room during peer editing sessions to make sure answers are being written down, to answer questions, to resolve disputes, and to encourage sharp thinking.

- Four appendices have been added for students' easy reference:

   Correction Symbols
   Kinds of Sentences
   Connectors
   Summary of Punctuation Rules

- The unit on business letters has been deleted to make space for a new section on using and punctuating quotations.

We have made these changes in response to the comments of reviewers and our colleagues who have used the first edition over the years. We hope that you will enjoy teaching from the new book and that your students will have fun learning from it.

To the Student

The most important aspect of a college education is to learn to communicate clearly and effectively. That is why general college education prerequisites include a number of composition and reading courses that you must complete before you can graduate.

Writing courses are essential because no matter what major you choose, you will be responsible for numerous papers in most of your classes. By taking reading and composition classes, you learn to analyze and understand required readings and discover ideas that you can use for writing assignments and projects.

Learning to write well is a step-by-step process. With each writing course you take, you will add to and improve your writing skills. The ability to write is not a talent one is born with. You can learn to write well if you try hard and complete each assignment to the best of your ability by spending considerable time and effort on it.

The purpose of this book is to teach some basic academic writing skills. They include a variety of organizational patterns, selected grammatical structures and sentence structures, and the steps in the writing process. As you learn to apply all of these skills to your writing, your papers will improve, and you will develop more confidence in your ability to write.

Each time you work on and complete an assignment, you will have added another building block to strengthen your foundation as a writer. So, get started and meet the challenges presented in this book, and you will soon be on your way to writing well.

Acknowledgments

We would like to express our sincere appreciation to all of those people who have helped to shape this edition. First and foremost, we would like to thank Allen Ascher of Addison Wesley Longman, whose guidance, invaluable suggestions, and constant feedback helped us in writing the second edition. We also owe a special debt to Liza Pleva, our production editor; Amy Durfy, our photo researcher; and Kathleen Schultz, our copyeditor. We also thank Joe Starr of Houston Community College and Grazyna Kenda of Technical Center Institute for their many helpful comments and suggestions. Moreover, our special thanks go to Caroline Gibbs of the Intensive English Program at the College of Marin and Cynthia Weber of the Berkeley Adult School as well as Patricia McEvoy Jamil and Victor Turks of City College of San Francisco for their advice and for trying out and critiquing new material for us. Finally, we thank our students, who were a constant inspiration to us.

Unit 1 Writing About People

PREWRITING
- *Asking Questions and Taking Notes*

ORGANIZATION
- *Finished Paragraph Format*

  Title Rules

GRAMMAR AND MECHANICS
- *Capitalization Rules*
- *End-of-Sentence Punctuation Rules*

SENTENCE STRUCTURE
- *Simple Sentences/Parts of a Sentence*
- *Subject-Verb Agreement*

  Prepositional Phrases

THE WRITING PROCESS

Writing is a progressive activity. This means that when you first write something down, you have already been thinking about what you are going to say and how you are going to say it. Then after you have finished writing, you read over what you have written and make changes and corrections. Therefore, writing is never a one-step action; it is a process that has several steps.

Prewriting: Asking Questions and Taking Notes

Prewriting is the first step in the writing process. In this step, you gather ideas to write about. One way to gather ideas is to discuss a topic with your classmates and take notes.

ACTIVITY 1

Work with a partner or a small group.

A. Look at the pictures of Madonna and Michael Jordan. Discuss the following questions, and take notes on your discussion on the lines that follow in Part B.

1. What kind of work does this person do?

2. How old is he (she)?

3. Where does he (she) live?

4. What other facts do you know about this person?

5. What outstanding characteristic or ability does this person have?

6. What unfavorable quality (if any) does this person have?

7. How has this person influenced other people in either a positive or a negative way?

8. Which age group of people admires this person the most?

9. Do you admire him (her)? Why or why not?

Madonna

Michael Jordan

B. On the lines below, take notes on your discussion. Write down what you and your classmate(s) know about this person's life, abilities, and accomplishments. Also, write down any reasons you and your classmate(s) have for admiring or not admiring this person.

NOTES

_____

_____

_____

_____

_____

_____

_____

_____

 **ACTIVITY 2**

A. In the picture frame below, draw a picture of one person whom you admire. This person might be a world leader, a person from history, a national hero from your country, a sports star, a well-known entertainer, a family member such as your mother or grandfather, a teacher, or a close friend.

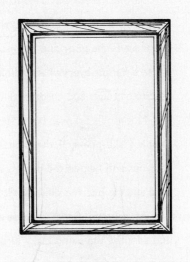

_____
(Name of person)

B. Prepare to talk about the person you have drawn by making notes on the lines below. Use the list of questions from Activity 1 on page 2. Add any other information that you feel is important.

NOTES

_____

_____

_____

_____

C. Work with a partner or a small group. Take turns telling your classmate(s) about the person you have drawn. Do not read your answers from your notes but refer to them as you talk naturally. Of course, your classmate(s) may ask additional questions.

D. Save your notes. You will use them later to write a paragraph.

MODEL ESSAY:
Writing About People

As you read the model essay, notice the capitalized words and the subject-verb agreement.

Mother of Hope

Mother Teresa was a Roman Catholic nun[1] in Calcutta, India. She worked with many nuns who belong to the Order[2] of the Missionaries of Charity.[3] The order feeds the poor and has established schools, orphanages,[4] and youth centers. People everywhere admired Mother Teresa for her dedication to

5   destitute[5] adults and children all over the world.

Mother Teresa was born Agnes Gonxha Bojaxhiu on August 27, 1910, in Skopje ("sko-pee-ay"), the capital city of Macedonia. Her family was very religious and helped the hungry and homeless. When she was nine, her father died and life became difficult. However, the family was happy and full of love.

10   At eighteen, Agnes became a nun at the Loreto Abbey in Dublin, Ireland, and adopted the name Mary Teresa. A few months later, she became a teacher at the Loreto Convent School in Calcutta, India, where she taught the daughters

---

[1]**nun:** woman member of a Christian religious group; [2]**order:** group of people who live under the same religious rules; [3]**Missionaries of Charity:** group of people who help the poor; [4]**orphanage:** home for children without a parent/parents; [5]**destitute:** lacking the simple necessities of life: food, clothing, and shelter

of wealthy people. Later, she was named the principal of the school and was called Mother Teresa.

15   In 1948, Mother Teresa left the order to live among and to help the poorest people in Calcutta. After she learned about the illnesses of the poor, she started to work with the Missionaries of Charity and medical professionals who had volunteered their help. Subsequently, her work expanded to ninety-five countries, including Venezuela, Italy, Tanzania, Great Britain, Australia,

20   and the United States.

Mother Teresa was admired all over the world for her work. In 1979, she was awarded the Nobel Peace Prize in Norway. Young Norwegians presented her with thousands of dollars they had collected to help her in her work. At Harvard University graduation ceremonies, Mother Teresa received an honorary award.

25   The day before the ceremony, she spoke to the graduates, who listened with great respect and gave her a standing ovation.[6] In November 1995, in a ceremony at St. Paul's Church in San Francisco, thirty nuns became volunteers[7] for Mother Teresa. Indeed, Mother Teresa was respected by people in all walks of life.[8]

Mother Teresa died on September 6, 1997 at the age of 87. Mother Teresa

30   had spent most of her life caring for the forgotten people of the world. She felt unworthy of the many honors she had received. However, they enabled her to raise funds to continue her fine work among the destitute, and for that, she was truly grateful.

QUESTIONS ON THE MODEL

1. What is the main idea of the essay about Mother Teresa?

2. Which paragraph discusses Mother Teresa's charitable work?

3. Which paragraph discusses the world's recognition of her work?

4. How many examples are given of Mother Teresa's recognition by the world community?

5. Look at the final paragraph.

   a. Which sentence makes a statement about her honors?

   b. Which sentences refer to her work?

   c. Which sentence explains Mother Teresa's gratitude?

---

[6]**ovation:** loud clapping hands to express welcome or approval; [7]**volunteer:** person who offers one's services to help without payment or reward; [8]**walk of life:** a particular social position in life, occupation

PART *1* Organization

A **paragraph** is a group of related statements that a writer develops about a subject. The first sentence states the specific point, or idea, of the topic. The rest of the sentences in the paragraph support that point, or idea.

An **essay** is a piece of writing that has more than one paragraph. It is divided into three parts: a beginning, a middle, and an end. The beginning is called the *introduction,* the middle is called the *body,* and the end is called the *conclusion.* The introduction and the conclusion are usually one paragraph each. The body may have from one to an unlimited number of paragraphs.

Each paragraph is a separate unit that is marked by indenting the first word from the left-hand margin or, as shown in the essay about Mother Teresa, by leaving extra space above and below the paragraph.

For example, the essay about Mother Teresa has six paragraphs. The first paragraph is the introduction. It names the topic of the essay, Mother Teresa. It describes Mother Teresa's life and her work at the order with the other nuns. The last paragraph is the conclusion. It brings the essay to a close and ends with the writer's final thoughts to give the reader something to think about. The second through fourth paragraphs in the middle are the body, which develops the main points of the essay.

Each body paragraph discusses a different feature of the subject.

- Paragraph 2 (the first body paragraph) tells about Mother Teresa's early life at home with her family.

- Paragraph 3 (the second body paragraph) tells about her decision to become a nun and her positions as teacher and principal.

- Paragraph 4 (the third body paragraph) describes her life and work with the poor and sick people in Calcutta, India.

- Paragraph 5 (the fourth body paragraph) explains people's admiration for Mother Teresa and the awards she had received.

Finished Paragraph Format

Here are some important instructions to follow when you handwrite or type essay assignments for this course. Your instructor may add other instructions.

Handwritten Paragraph

1. Use 8½-inch by 11-inch lined, three-hole binder paper. The three holes should be on your left side as you write. Write on one side of the paper only.

2. Write your name in the top right corner.

3. Center the title on the top line.

4. Leave one blank line, and start your paragraph on the third line.

5. Indent one inch from the left margin to begin the paragraph.

6. Leave the left and right margins blank. Do not write in the margins.

7. Leave a blank line between each line of writing.

8. Leave the bottom line blank.

Typed Paragraph

1. Use 8½-inch by 11-inch white paper. Type on one side of the paper only.

2. Type your name in the top right corner.

3. Center the title about 1½ inches from the top edge of the paper.

4. Leave four blank lines between the title and the first line of your paragraph.

5. Indent five spaces to begin the paragraph.

6. Leave one-inch margins on both sides and the bottom of the paper. Do not type in the margins.

7. Double space. (Leave one blank line between each line of typing.)

Title Rules

A **title** is used to attract attention and generally tells the reader what to expect. It is usually a phrase, not a sentence.

Although a one-paragraph composition does not require a title, you should use one for each writing assignment. A title will help you keep your mind on the topic as you write.

RULES	EXAMPLES
1. Capitalize the first, last, and important words in a title.	**C**hoosing a **V**acation **S**pot
2. Do not capitalize short prepositions such as *on, to, in,* and *for;* short conjunctions such as *and, or,* and *so;* and the articles *a, an,* and *the.*	**H**ow to **F**ight **S**tress **W**inning the **L**ottery
EXCEPTION: Capitalize a short word if it is the first word in a title.	**T**he **P**roblems of **S**ingle **P**arenting **T**he **A**dvantages of **P**ublic **T**ransportation

Kazumi Ito

A Future Businessman

I would like to introduce my classmate

Roberto Sanchez. He is from the beautiful island of

Puerto Rico in the Caribbean Sea. Roberto is twenty-one

years old. He was born in San Juan, the capital city.

His native language is Spanish, but he studied English

in school. Roberto comes from a large family. He has

three older brothers and two younger sisters. He likes

to play the guitar and sing Spanish folk songs.

Baseball is his favorite sport. Now he is studying

English at Greenhill College. Then he will major in

business at a university. After graduation, he will

become a businessman in Puerto Rico. Good luck, Roberto!

Muhammad Kureshi

1½" margin

Center title   **A Troubled Leader**   *1" margin*

1" margin   *Leave 4 blank lines*

Indent 5 spaces   Benazir Bhutto was the first woman ever to serve as prime   *Double space*
minister in Pakistan, an Islamic nation. She was prime minister from
1988 until 1990 and became prime minister again in 1993. Prime
Minister Bhutto was born in Karachi on June 21, 1953. She received
her higher education at Harvard University in the United States and
at Oxford University in England. Then she returned to Pakistan in
1977. Her father, Zulfikar Ali Bhutto, was president and prime minister.
However, he was forcefully removed from power by General Zia and
sent to prison, where he was executed in 1979. Immediately
afterward, Benazir Bhutto was placed under house arrest. She
remained there for nine years. In 1987, she married a wealthy man in
a marriage arranged by her family and is the mother of three children.
After General Zia's death in 1988, Bhutto led the Pakistan People's
Party (PPP) to victory and became prime minister. Then in August
1990, Pakistan's President Khan charged Bhutto's government with
corruption, and she was removed from office. Soon after, she won a
seat in parliament, and in 1993, Bhutto was reelected prime minister.
Subsequently, Bhutto and her government were again charged with
corruption. President Leghari dismissed her from office in 1996. At
this time, her future role in Pakistani politics is unclear.

1" margin

PART **2** Grammar and Mechanics

Capitalization

In English there are many rules for using capital letters. You probably know many of them already. To test your knowledge, look at the essay about Mother Teresa on pages 4–5 again, and write the words with capital letters on the lines that follow. Add the rules (if you know them) to the right of the words.

1. _____

2. _____

3. _____

4. _____

   (Continue on a separate sheet of paper.)

You may not have been able to give all the rules, but aren't you surprised at how many you already know?

Capitalization Rules

Here are some important rules for capitalization.

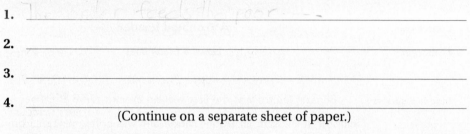

RULES	**EXAMPLES**
Capitalize:	
I. The first word of a sentence.	**M**other Teresa is admired for her work all over the world.
2. The pronoun *I*.	The nuns and **I** try to care for poor, sick people throughout the world.
3. Abbreviations and acronyms, which are words formed from the first letters of the words in the names of organizations.	**FBI IBM AIDS** **USA YMCA WHO** **UN DDT** **UNICEF**
4. All proper nouns. Proper nouns include	
a. Names of deities.	**G**od **A**llah **S**hiva
b. Names of people and their titles.	**J**ane **P. D**oe, **Ph.D.** **D**iana, **P**rincess of **W**ales **D**r. **J**onas **S**alk **P**rofessor **H**enry **H**iggins **M**r. and **M**rs. **J**ohn **O. S**mith
BUT NOT a title without a name.	the general, the prime minister, the math professor, the prince, the king

c.	Names of specific places you could find on a map.	**G**ary, **I**ndiana **L**ake **V**ictoria **M**editerranean **S**ea **T**elegraph **A**venue **N**orth **P**ole **T**rafalgar **S**quare **F**irst **S**treet
d.	Names of days, months, and special days.	**M**onday **I**ndependence **D**ay **J**anuary **R**amadan

BUT NOT the names of the seasons.

e.	Names of specific groups of people (nationalities, races, and ethnic groups), languages, and religions.	**A**sian **R**ussian **C**aucasian **M**oslem **A**merican **E**nglish **J**ehovah's **W**itness **A**rabic
f.	Names of geographic areas.	the **M**iddle **E**ast the **S**outhwest the **N**orth **J**ane's home is in the **S**outh, but **T**om comes from the **E**ast **C**oast.

BUT NOT the names of compass directions.

Drive east for two blocks, and then turn south.

g.	Names of school subjects with course numbers.	**B**usiness **A**dministration 17**B** **G**erman 101 **C**hemistry 10**A**

BUT NOT names of classes without numbers, except languages.

computer science, business administration, economics, **G**erman conversation, **E**nglish composition

h.	Names of specific structures such as buildings and bridges.	**G**olden **G**ate **B**ridge **P**ark **P**laza **H**otel the **W**hite **H**ouse **K**ensington **P**alace
i.	Names of specific organizations (businesses, clubs, schools).	**S**ears, **R**oebuck & **C**o. **S**umitomo **B**ank **I**nternational **S**tudents' **C**lub **U**niversity of **C**alifornia **S**t. **M**ary's **H**igh **S**chool **A**merican **H**eart **A**ssociation
j.	Titles of compositions, stories, books, magazines, newspapers, plays, poems, and movies.	*Introducing Myself* *Introduction to Academic Writing* *All Quiet on the Western Front* *Star Wars*

NOTE: Underline or italicize the titles of books, magazines, newspapers, plays, and movies.

PRACTICE:
Capitalization

A. Change small letters to capital letters wherever it is necessary in the following sentences.

1. farnaz is a student from iran. she speaks english, french, and farsi. her major is chemistry.

2. three important winter holidays in the united states are christmas, hanukkah, and new year's day.

3. president john f. kennedy was born on may 29, 1917, and was assassinated[1] on november 22, 1963.

4. greenhills college is located in boston, massachusetts.

5. i am taking four classes this semester: english 40, sociology 32, typing, and a computer science course.

6. thanksgiving is always on the fourth thursday in november.

7. excuse me! can you please tell me where the golden gate bridge is?

8. there are three main religions in japan: buddhism, shintoism, and christianity.

9. i work during the months of june, july, and august.

10. i read a good book last weekend called *the old man and the sea* by ernest hemingway.

B. Change small letters to capital letters wherever it is necessary in the following essay.

A Dedicated[2] Scientist

rachel l. carson was a famous american writer and marine biologist. she was born on may 27, 1907, on a farm in pennsylvania. as a child, rachel loved to take walks with her mother in the woods and fields. they enjoyed identifying and listening to birds and small animals. rachel also had other interests. she loved to read and write. nature was her favorite subject. as a preteen, she wrote stories, and some appeared in a magazine.

ms. carson was an excellent student in high school. after she graduated, she entered pennsylvania college for women in pittsburgh to major in english. however, she changed her major to science and graduated with highest honors in may 1929. she then studied at johns hopkins university in maryland and received a master's degree in marine zoology.[3] after her education, she worked for the u.s. bureau of

---

[1]**assassinated:** murdered; [2]**dedicated:** devoted to some work; [3]**marine zoology:** the scientific study of sea animals

fisheries. at first, she was hired as a writer on marine life. later, she received an appointment as a biologist, and she continued to write.

in 1951, rachel carson wrote the sea around us. it was about the formation of the sea and the life in it. soon after, she published several more books about the sea. in 1962, silent spring was published. it was about the irresponsible[4] use of pesticides.[5] according to ms. carson, pesticides were destroying the environment by poisoning the soil and seas. she wrote that people and animals were becoming sick, too. the book became a best-seller and was published in many languages. it resulted in the worldwide ban[6] on the use of DDT.

on april 14, 1964, rachel carson died of cancer. she cared about the environment and wanted to preserve the earth, oceans, and all living things. she was a very concerned scientist and writer and a remarkable human being.

c. With a partner, take turns reading a sentence from the essay about Rachel Carson. Give the capitalization rule for each capital letter in the sentence.

Punctuation

Punctuation is necessary to make sentence meaning clear. The meanings of the following two sentences are different:

> Stop Bill!
> Stop, Bill!

The first sentence tells someone to stop Bill. The second sentence tells Bill to stop.

---

[4]**irresponsible:** not caring about the effects; [5]**pesticide:** chemical substance used to kill small animals or insects; [6]**ban:** an order forbidding something

End-of-Sentence Punctuation Rules

There are three punctuation marks that you can use at the end of a sentence: the *period*, the *question mark*, and the *exclamation mark*.

RULES   **EXAMPLES**

1. Put a period (full stop) at the end of a statement.   My name is Jennifer Wong.
I don't like to give interviews.

2. Put a question mark at the end of a question.   What is your name?
Do you speak English?

3. Put an exclamation mark at the end of a sentence to show strong feeling.   It sure is hot today!
I'm crazy about soccer!

CAUTION: Do not overuse exclamation marks. To understand why you should not, compare these two paragraphs:

The telephone rang at midnight! I ran to answer it! I didn't hear a voice! I said, "Hello! Hello!" There was no answer! I was frightened!

The telephone rang at midnight. I ran to answer it. I didn't hear a voice. I said, "Hello? Hello?" There was no answer. I was frightened!

The first paragraph has too many exclamation marks. The second paragraph, with only one exclamation mark at the end of the last sentence to show strong feeling, is more effective.

WRITING PRACTICE: *About Yourself*

Write a paragraph about yourself. Use the answers to the following questions as a basis for your writing. Add any additional information you wish, for example, information about your job or hobbies.

- Be careful to end each sentence with a period.
- Practice the rules for capitalization.

    1. What is your full name? (first, middle, family name)
    2. Where are you from? (city and country)
    3. What languages do you speak?
    4. What important holidays do you have in your country?
    5. What is the name of your school or college?
    6. What are your favorite school subjects?

- With a partner, edit and revise your paragraph. Check your own and your partner's paragraph especially for correct format, punctuation, and capitalization.

PART 3 Sentence Structure

Simple Sentences/ Parts of a Sentence

A **sentence** is a group of words that contains at least one subject and one verb. A sentence expresses a complete thought.

There are four kinds of sentences in English: *simple* sentences, *compound* sentences, *complex* sentences, and *compound-complex* sentences. First, we will learn about simple sentences.

> A **simple sentence** has one subject and one verb. The **subject** tells *who* or *what* did something. The **verb** tells the action (or condition).

These are simple sentences:

Subject	Verb
I	study.
I	study and work.
My head	hurts.
My head and neck	hurt.
It	is raining.
The students	are reading.

(Notice that the subject in a simple sentence may be compound: *My head and neck* hurt. Also, the verb in a simple sentence may be compound: I *study and work.*)

NOTE: "Save your money" is also a complete sentence. The subject "you" is understood and not included.

A sentence may also have a complement (but it does not *have* to have one). The **complement** completes the meaning of the verb or adds more information to the sentence. There are many types of complements. A complement in a simple sentence may be a noun, pronoun, adjective, or adverb.

Subject	Verb	Complement
I	study	English. (noun)
I	don't understand	you. (pronoun)
His girlfriend	is	smart. (adjective)
It	isn't raining	now. (adverb)

A complement may also be a noun phrase, a verb phrase, or a prepositional phrase.

My father	owns	his own business. (noun phrase)
My girlfriend	wants	to get married. (verb phrase)
The students	are reading	in the library. (prepositional phrase)

A complement may also be a combination.

| I | study | English at Greenhills College. (noun + prepositional phrase) |
| She | wants | to get married soon. (verb phrase + adverb) |

Subject-Verb Agreement

You already know that subjects and verbs must agree in number.

> My *sister is* married. **(singular)**
> My *sisters are* married. **(plural)**
> My *brother and my sister are* single. **(plural)**

Sometimes students make mistakes in subject-verb agreement when the subject has a prepositional phrase following it. For this reason, you should learn to recognize prepositional phrases.

Prepositional Phrases

> A **prepositional phrase** is a group of words that begins with a preposition and ends with a pronoun, noun, or noun phrase.

Prepositional phrases express time, place, possession, and some other things. A prepositional phrase usually tells where, when, how, why, or whose.

from Mexico City	in the morning
on January 1	of my sisters
to my best friend	around the room
by bus	because of the weather
after her	at himself

A prepositional phrase may come after the subject of a sentence, but *it is not part of the subject.* Therefore, you should ignore[1] it most of the time when you are trying to decide which verb form to use.

> One (of my sisters) is also a singer.

(The subject is *one,* which is singular.)
Here are some other examples:

Singular subjects
One (of my brothers) is a musician.
Neither (of my parents) is living.
Much (of my time) is spent in the library.
Each (of my brothers) wants his own car.
Either (of my sisters) is able to baby-sit for you tonight.

Plural subjects
Both (of my parents) are teachers.
Several (of the teachers) speak my language.

Unfortunately, telling a singular subject from a plural subject isn't always easy. A few words can be either singular or plural. In these cases, you must refer to the noun in the prepositional phrase.

> Some (of the money) was missing. (singular)
> Some (of the students) were missing. (plural)

> All (of my time) is spent in the library. (singular)
> All (of my brothers) are singers. (plural)

---

[1]**ignore:** pay no attention to

Most (of the ice) was melted. (singular)
Most (of the ice cubes) were melted. (plural)

A lot (of the work) was too easy. (singular)
A lot (of the people) were angry. (plural)

None (of the fruit) is fresh. (singular)
None (of the apples) are fresh. (plural)

*Identifying
Subjects, Verbs,
and Complements*

Underline the subjects, verbs, and complements in the following sentences and write S, V, or C above them. Also put parentheses ( ) around prepositional phrases.

1. My name is Roberto Sanchez.

2. I was born (on September 21, 1978) (in the city) (of San Juan, Puerto Rico.)

3. I am a student at Greenhills College in Boston, Massachusetts.

4. Some of my classes are difficult.

5. Some of the homework is boring.

6. None of my classmates speak Spanish.

7. A lot of my classes are in Dante Hall.

8. A lot of my time is spent in the student lounge.

9. My father works in an office.

10. None of us are married.

11. My youngest brother and sister are still in high school.

12. My father understands English but doesn't speak it.

13. In my country, most of the people are Catholic.

14. Neither of my parents has been to the United States.

PRACTICE:
*Subject-Verb
Agreement*

Complete the essay with the correct verb forms. Put parentheses ( ) around prepositional phrases.

A Courageous Man

Christopher Reeve _____is_____ a famous Hollywood actor. He
            1. be

played the role of Superman in several movies. Some of his other

movies _____ Deathtrap, The Bostonian, and The Remains of
        2. include

the Day.

(continued on the next page)

Reeve was also an experienced horseback rider. However, on May 27, 1995, while he was performing in a riding competition, his horse stopped suddenly. He was thrown off and hit his head on the ground. Tragically, he suffered serious injuries and _____ now
3. be
paralyzed.[1] Reeve _____ unable to use his arms and legs. He
4. be
_____ around in a motorized wheelchair. He cannot breathe
5. get
without the aid of a respirator.[2] He also _____ a neck
6. wear
support. At first, he could not eat solid food, but now he can.

Reeve _____ a strong support system. His loving family and
7. have
friends _____ there for him. During his hospital stay, his wife,
8. be
Dana, visited him and often brought along their young son, Will. One of
his Hollywood friends _____ comedian Robin Williams. Williams's
9. be
funny jokes _____ him _____ and _____ his
10. make   11. laugh   12. lift
spirits. A lot of Americans and people around the world have sent him
cards, letters, and telegrams of encouragement and best wishes.

Reeve _____ truly grateful to everyone. He _____
13. be   14. be
thankful for the excellent medical care he received from the medical
staff at the hospital. His doctor _____ him a courageous man
15. call
and a wonderful patient. He was released from the hospital in December
1995. Then on March 25, 1996, Reeve made a surprise appearance at
the Academy Award ceremonies in Hollywood and made a speech.

Reeve _____ a strong will to live as normal a life as
16. have
possible. Pictures of his smiling, handsome face _____ his
17. show
positive attitude. All of Reeve's friends and supporters _____
18. hope
and _____ for his recovery.
19. pray

---

[1]**paralyzed:** lost the ability to move; [2]**respirator:** device to help a person to breathe

WRITING
PRACTICE: *About Your Family*

Write a composition of three paragraphs about your family. Write one paragraph about your father, one paragraph about your mother, and one paragraph about your siblings.[3]

- In your first paragraph, write about your father. You might begin the first paragraph with a general sentence like these:

   or My father is the head of our family.
   My father is a very interesting person.

Use these questions to help you write about him. (You do not have to answer every question. They are intended only to give you ideas to write about.) Add other information if you wish.

1. What is your father's name?

2. Where was he born?

3. How old is he?

4. What is his occupation?

5. What is his role in the family?

6. How does he spend his leisure time?

7. What do you think of your father?

- In your second paragraph, write about your mother. Answer the same questions to write about her.
- In your third paragraph, write about your siblings.

1. How many brothers do you have? How many sisters?

2. Are they younger or older than you?

3. How old are they?

4. Are they students, or are they out of school? Explain.

5. What is your relationship with them?

6. How are they different from each other?

- Use sentence structures with prepositional phrases such as *one of my brothers is* and *all of my sisters are.*
- With a partner, edit and revise your paragraph. Check your own and your partner's paragraphs, especially for correct format, punctuation, and capitalization.

---

[3]**sibling:** brother or sister

PART 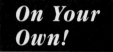 The Writing Process

On Your Own!

Now let's complete the writing process you began at the beginning of the unit. Write a composition of one or more paragraphs about the person whom you admire. Follow these steps to write a good composition.

STEP 1:
Prewrite to Get Ideas

At the beginning of the unit, you made notes from the list of questions on page 2. You also made notes as your classmate(s) asked you questions and commented on the person you admired.

STEP 2:
Organize the Ideas

Make a list of the ideas in the order that you will write about them. You will use this list to guide you as you write.

STEP 3:
Write the Rough Draft

Write ROUGH DRAFT at the top of your paper.

- Begin your composition with a sentence that names the person you admire.

  Benito Juarez was a great Mexican leader.

  Everyone in my hometown looks up to my grandfather.

  Madonna is a singer who has the courage to be different.

- Then use your notes to write a rough draft of a composition about the person you admire. Use specific examples of admirable behavior or accomplishments. If you need more information about a well-known person, go to the library reference section.

- End your composition with a sentence that tells why this person is admirable.

  Benito Juarez is a great hero in my country because he was for the people.

  My grandfather is respected because he has spent all his life helping others.

  Madonna is my personal heroine because she does not worry about what other people think.

MODEL:
Rough Draft

Here is a rough draft of a student composition titled "My Brother Ryan." Notice that it contains many errors.

My Brother Ryan

    I admire my brother Ryan a lot. He's twenty-two years old and goes to Creighton University in New York. I'm four years younger. He was good athletic in school. When we were kids we had a lots of fun together. He was on the community swim team. He swims fast. He often win the first place. Ryan played

5   soccer on the city team. He was ten years old. He was the best team player. His team lost the championship by one point. I was sad, but he said that other team was better. He was good athletic. He encourage me to join swim team too. I could swim fast, but I didn't win many first-place ribbon. Mostly second or third place. But he alway rooted[1] for me. In high school, he loved to play

10   basketball. His team played many high school team and won. I wanted to play basketball too. He practised shooting baskets with me a lot. My brother told me to play sports because they teach you many good things. For example, team sports teach you good sportsmanship.[2] You have to cooperate with your team if you want to win. If your team loses, you must not get angry. You just

15   have to remember to play the best you can. I really admire my brother Ryan a lot because he is good athletic, he is wise, and he is my good friend.

STEP 4:
Edit the Rough Draft

First, use the Editing Checklist on the next page and edit your paragraph by answering the Writer's Questions. Then ask a classmate, the peer editor, to read your paragraph and complete the Peer Editor's Answers and Comments section of the checklist. The peer editor should suggest ways to improve your composition.

---

[1]**rooted:** applauded, cheered, encouraged; [2]**sportsmanship:** good behavior, fairness

EDITING CHECKLIST

Writer's Questions	Peer Editor's Answers and Comments
FORMAT	
1. Does the composition have a title?	yes no
2. Is each paragraph indented?	yes no
3. Are there margins on both sides?	yes no
4. Is the composition double-spaced?	yes no
ORGANIZATION	
5. Does the composition have more than one paragraph?	How many paragraphs are there? What is the topic of each paragraph?
6. If the composition has more than one paragraph, are the paragraphs divided logically?	
GRAMMAR AND MECHANICS	
7. Is there a period at the end of each sentence?	Check each sentence. Does each one end with a period? yes no Add any missing periods.
8. Are capital letters used where necessary?	Write down any words that should be capitalized and are not.
SENTENCE STRUCTURE	
9. Does each sentence have a subject and a verb and express a complete thought?	Check each sentence. Underline any sentences that you have doubts about.
10. Does each verb agree with its subject?	Write down any subjects and verbs that do not agree.
11. Did you use prepositional phrases?	Write down any prepositional phrases used in the composition.

MODEL:
*Edited and
Revised Draft*

Here is the composition "My Brother Ryan" after the student writer self-edited the rough draft on page 21:

My Brother Ryan

I admire my brother Ryan a lot. He's twenty-two years old and goes to Creighton University in New York. I'm four years younger. He was ~~good athletic~~ *a athlete* in school. ~~When we were kids we had a lots of fun together.~~ He was on the community swim team. He ~~swims~~ *swam* fast. He often ~~win~~ *won* the first place. Ryan *also* played soccer on the city team. He was ten years old. ~~He~~ *and* was the best team player. His team lost the championship by one point. I was sad, but ~~he said that~~ *the* other team was better. ~~He was good athletic.~~ He encourage*d* me to join *the* swim team, too. I could swim fast, but I didn't win many first-place ribbon*s* Mostly *I won* second or third place. But he always*s* rooted for me. In high school, he loved to play basketball. His team played many ~~high school~~ team*s* and won. I wanted to play basketball, too. He practi*c*ed shooting baskets with me a lot. My brother told me to play sports because they teach you many good things. For example, team sports teach you good sportsmanship. You have to cooperate with your team if you want to win. If your team loses, you must not get angry. You just have to remember to play the best you can. I really ~~admire~~ *look up to* my brother ~~Ryan~~ a lot. ~~because he~~ *He* is *a* good ~~athletic~~ *athlete*, he is wise, and he is *also* my good friend.

STEP 5:
*Write the Second
Draft*

Write SECOND DRAFT at the top of your paper. Write the second draft of your composition to hand in to your instructor.

STEP 6:
Write the Final Draft

After your instructor returns your composition with his/her comments and corrections, write a neat final copy to hand in for final evaluation. Write FINAL DRAFT at the top of your paper.

ADDITIONAL WRITING

1. Write a composition about a neighbor or teacher whom you disliked.

   Ms. Humbug, my neighbor, is mean to young people.

   My sixth-grade teacher, Mr. Lemon, was the most hated teacher in our school.

2. Write a composition about one of your classmates. First, interview him or her to find out some facts about his/her background, family, hobbies, interests, job, or plans for the future. Avoid asking questions about age, religion, money, or other personal topics.

Unit 2 Narration

توصيف - داستان گويى

*I*n this unit, you will concentrate on writing **narration,** a kind of writing in which you report events. In the first part of the unit, you will write about an event or experience that happened to you in the past. In the second part, you will write about the traditional events of a wedding.

Prewriting: Freewriting

Freewriting is a way first to get and then to develop ideas. When you freewrite, you write "freely"—without stopping—on a topic for a specific amount of time. You just write down sentences as you think of them without worrying about whether your sentences are correct or not. You also don't have to punctuate sentences or capitalize words. You can even write incomplete sentences or phrases. The main goal in freewriting is to keep your pencil moving across the paper.

Look at this example of freewriting on the topic "A Memorable Event in My Life."

MODEL:
Freewriting

A Memorable Event in My Life

I'm supposed to freewrite for ten minutes about a memorable event in my life. I don't know what to write about. Maybe about my brother's boat accident. We were so scared. We thought he was going to drown. He was trapped under an overturned boat and didn't have any air to breathe. But it ended all right.

5 He was rescued and only had a broken arm. What else can I write about? Oh! I know. A day I will always remember was the day I left my country to come to the United States. That was a sad/happy day. I felt sad and happy at the same time. Maybe I should write about something happy. Our family vacation last summer was fun. We drove to the coast and camped for a week on the

10 beach. Then there was the day the earthquake happened. Now <u>that</u> was definitely a memorable event. I will never forget it. I was at home with my older sister and little brother. . . .

This writer freewrote until he found a good topic: the earthquake. If he had wanted to, he could have done further freewriting about his earthquake experience to develop this topic.

ACTIVITY

Now you try it. Freewrite about a memorable event or experience in your life. This might be a happy day, a sad event, an embarrassing moment, an interesting trip, or a frightening experience. Write for about ten minutes without stopping. If you find a topic during your freewriting, continue freewriting on that topic. If you already have a topic in mind before you start, freewrite on that topic for ten minutes to develop your ideas about it.

Save your freewriting. You will use it later to write a paragraph.

MODEL ESSAY:
Narration

As you read the model essay, look for words and phrases that show time order.

Earthquake!

October 17, 1989, was a day that I will never forget. It was the day I experienced my first earthquake. I had just gotten home from school and was lying on the living room sofa watching the news on TV. My little brother was in his room playing, and my older sister was in the kitchen preparing our dinner.
5 Our parents were still at work.

At exactly 5:04 P.M., the earthquake struck. Our apartment started shaking violently as if it were a small wooden boat being tossed by giant waves in the ocean. At first, none of us realized what was happening. Then my sister yelled, "Earthquake! Get under something!" I was too stunned[1] to move, but the
10 shaking was so strong that I soon fell off the sofa onto the floor. I half rolled, half crawled across the floor to the dining table and got under it. My sister was sitting on the floor in the kitchen, holding her arms over her head to protect it from falling dishes. She yelled at my little brother to get under his desk, but he wanted to be near us. He tried to get out of his room, but he kept falling down.
15 The earthquake lasted less than a minute, but it seemed like a year to us.

At last, the shaking stopped. For a minute or two, we were too scared to move. Then my sister and I cautiously got up and went to help our little brother, who was crying. As soon as he saw us, he began to calm down. There was no electricity, so I looked for my transistor radio and turned it on.
20 Unfortunately, it didn't work because the batteries were too old. Next, we checked the apartment for damage, but we didn't find any. We felt very lucky, for nothing was broken and no one was hurt. After a while, we started worrying about our parents. I tried to call them at work, but the phone lines were busy.

Two hours later, our parents finally arrived home. They were unhurt, but
25 they had had to walk home because the electric streetcars were not working. We were so happy to see them!

Our first earthquake was an experience that none of us will ever forget, but it taught us a lesson, too. Now we keep emergency supplies such as fresh batteries for my radio available, and we have an emergency plan for
30 communication with one another.

---

[1]**stunned:** very surprised, shocked

QUESTIONS ON THE MODEL

1. How many time divisions are in the model essay? What are they?

2. How many paragraphs are in the model essay? What time words or phrases begin each paragraph? Circle them.

PART *1* Organization

Narration: Time Order

Narration is story writing. When you write a narrative paragraph or essay, you write about events in the order that they happened. In other words, you use time order to organize your sentences.

In the model essay, the writer used time order to divide the essay into paragraphs. First, he wrote about what he and his family were doing just before the earthquake. Then he wrote about what happened during the earthquake. Next, he wrote about what they did immediately after the earthquake. In the fourth paragraph, he wrote about his parents' arrival home two hours later.

An outline of the essay would look like this:

I. Introduction: Before the earthquake

II. Body

    A. During the earthquake
    B. After the earthquake
    C. Two hours after the earthquake

III. Conclusion

Time Order Words and Phrases

Notice the kinds of words and phrases used to show time order. These are called time order words or phrases because they show the order in which events happen.

Words	Phrases
first (second, etc.)	at first
then	at exactly 5:04 P.M.
next	after a while
finally	after that
afterward	in the morning
meanwhile	in the meantime

Time order words and phrases are usually followed by a comma if they come at the beginning of a sentence. *Then* and *now* are usually not followed by a comma.

PRACTICE:
Time Order

A. Turn back to the model on page 26. Draw a circle around all of the time order words and phrases you find, and add any new ones to the list on page 27.

B. Complete the paragraphs with time order words and phrases from the lists provided and punctuate them correctly. Use each word or phrase once.

I. Use these words: *now, first, finally, then, next.*

How to Make Scrambled Eggs

Scrambled eggs are a quick and easy light meal. You need two fresh eggs, milk, butter, salt, and pepper. You also need a mixing bowl, a tablespoon, a fork, and a frying pan. _____First,_____ break the

a.
eggs into the bowl, and add about three tablespoons of milk and the salt and pepper. _____ beat the mixture with a fork until it is

b.
well mixed. _____ melt a small piece of butter in the frying pan

c.
over low heat. Pour the egg mixture into the pan, and let it heat through. _____ turn up the heat slightly, and as the eggs cook,

d.
push them around gently with the fork. When the scrambled eggs are done to perfection, they should be light and fluffy. _____ enjoy

e.
your delicious, healthful meal.

2. Use these words and phrases: *on the day of the party, during the party, before the party, at the beginning of the party, first, after that, then* (use twice), *next, finally, later.*

Fifteen Years

A girl's fifteenth birthday is a very special occasion in many Latin American countries and requires a lot of planning. _____

a.
the parents make many preparations. _____ they buy a special

b.
dress and order a bouquet of flowers for their daughter. They also plan a large meal for the guests and hire an orchestra. _____ they

c.
decorate a big room where the party will be held.

_____ there are many special traditions. _____ the
d.   e.

father and daughter enter the big salon accompanied by special music.

_____ the father makes a speech, and she gets some presents.
f.

_____ everyone drinks champagne. _____ the father and
g.   h.

daughter dance a waltz, and the daughter and every boy dance one

dance together. _____ all of the guests make a line to
i.

congratulate her. _____ all of the boys stand in a group because
j.

she will throw the bouquet, and the boy who catches it dances with

her. _____ everyone dances to different kinds of music until six
k.

o'clock in the morning.

c. The following sets of sentences are not in correct time order. Number the
sentences in the correct order.

1. _____ She put the clean dishes away.

_2_ She removed the dirty dishes from the table.

_____ She turned on the dishwasher.

_____ She put them in the dishwasher.

_____ She piled them in the sink and rinsed them.

_1_ It was Sarah's turn to wash the dishes last night.

_____ Finally, the dishes were clean.

2. _____ He filled it out and left.

_____ He went to the bookshelf, but the book wasn't there.

_____ Tom went to the library to get a book.

_____ He went to the computer catalog.

_____ The librarian told him to fill out a form.

_____ He told the librarian he wanted to reserve that book.

_____ He wrote down the title and call number of the book.

(continued on the next page)

3. _____ Our vacation in Florida last month was a real disaster.

   _____ On the way to the airport, our taxi broke down.

   _____ We got a new hotel room after arguing with the manager.

   _____ When we arrived back home, we found that water had flooded our house because of a broken pipe.

   _____ All in all, we should have stayed at home.

   _____ We had to wait several hours for the next flight.

   _____ When we arrived at our hotel in Miami, our reservations had been canceled because we were late.

   _____ It rained the entire week, so we couldn't go to the beach at all.

   _____ We missed our plane to Miami.

   _____ The second day we were in Miami, someone broke into our hotel room and stole all of our clothes.

WRITING PRACTICE:

Time Order Paragraph

Write the sentences from the preceding exercise as single paragraphs. Try to make your paragraphs flow smoothly by using these three techniques: (1) Add time order words or phrases at the beginning of some of the sentences. (2) Combine some of the sentences to form simple sentences with compound verbs. (3) Change nouns to pronouns where possible.

Example:

It was Sarah's turn to wash the dishes last night. First, she removed the dirty dishes from the table. Next, she piled them in the sink and rinsed them. After that, she put them in the dishwasher and turned it on. Finally, the dishes were clean, so she put them away.

PART 2 Grammar and Mechanics

MODEL ESSAY:
Simple Present Tense and Adverbs of Frequency

As you read the model essay, notice the verb tenses.

A Traditional Hindu Wedding

In every culture, weddings are important events. The families of both the bride and groom spend many months preparing for the big day. It is a joyous occasion when families and friends of the bride and groom gather for the solemn

marriage ceremony and stay to enjoy the festivities that follow it. In India,
traditional Hindu weddings are usually lavish[1] affairs with many special customs.

Several months before the wedding, the families of both the bride and
groom begin the preparations. The groom's family always buys jewelry for the
bride and gifts for the bride's family. They also buy the bride's wedding clothes,
which are traditionally red and gold in color. The groom gives her a necklace of
black beads called a *mangal sutra*, blessed thread. The bride never takes it off
while her husband is living. The bride's family always buys wedding clothes for
the groom, and they often provide a dowry.[2]

On the night before the ceremony, the bride's sisters traditionally paint
designs on the palms of her hands and on the soles[3] of her feet. They use a
natural dye from the henna plant. At first, the dye is green, but when she
washes her hands and feet the next morning, the designs turn bright red.

On the day of the ceremony, one of the groom's brothers goes to the
bride's home with gifts. These gifts seal the union of the two families. Then the
groom arrives at the bride's home with his family and his friends. He is dressed
in rich[4] clothing, and he wears a special headdress[5] and garlands[6] of flowers.
He usually arrives in a white car or on a white horse, but he sometimes rides
a white elephant to his wedding. Then the wedding ceremony takes place.

During the ceremony, the couple sits around a sacred fire under a special
canopy.[7] A Hindu priest performs the ceremony by chanting special wedding
prayers. After that, the bride's dress is tied to the groom's scarf, and they walk
around the fire seven times. The groom makes seven promises: to make his
wife happy, to share his feelings with her, to share his possessions with her, to
be faithful, to respect her family, and to make her a part of his life. The seventh
promise is to keep the other six promises!

The party begins after the ceremony. Musicians provide entertainment,
and a feast of traditional Indian food is served. During the party, the bride,
groom, and their guests play some traditional games. The party seldom ends
before midnight.

---

[1]**lavish:** expensive, grand; [2]**dowry:** money or property brought by a bride to her husband at marriage; [3]**sole:** bottom (of the foot); [4]**rich:** beautiful, expensive; [5]**headdress:** covering for the head; [6]**garland:** long ropes; [7]**canopy:** tent without walls

On the morning after the wedding, the bride leaves her family's house and goes with her new husband to his family's house. It is both a happy and a sad day. It is happy because two families are joining together and a young couple is beginning a new life. It is also sad because the bride is leaving her parents to become part of her husband's family.

35

SOURCE: Kalman, Bobbie. *India: The People*. New York: Crabtree Publishing Company, 1990.

QUESTIONS ON THE MODEL

1. How many paragraphs does the model essay have? How are they organized? (What kind of order?)

2. What is the main topic of each paragraph? List them here:

_____   _____

_____   _____

_____   _____

_____

3. What time order words or phrases are used to introduce time division? Circle them, and add any new ones to the list on page 27.

Simple Present Tense and Adverbs of Frequency

The **simple present tense** is the verb tense used to state facts and describe repeated activities.

In the model essay about a traditional Hindu wedding, the writer used the simple present tense because she wrote about events that traditionally happen again and again.

They also <u>buy</u> the bride's wedding clothes.

Remember to add -s when the subject is third-person singular *he, she,* or *it.*

The groom <u>gives</u> her a necklace of black beads.

Adverbs of frequency are words such as *always, usually, sometimes,* and *seldom.* These words tell how often something happens.

Position of Adverbs of Frequency

Place an adverb of frequency

1. Before the main verb.

The bride never takes it off.

2. After the verb *be* and all helping verbs in positive sentences: *am, are, is, was, were, have, has, had, do, does, did, shall, should, can, could, will, would, may, might,* or *must.*

    Traditional Hindu weddings are usually lavish affairs.

3. If the helping verb is negative—*isn't, doesn't, won't,* and so on—the word order is as follows:

    a. The adverbs *sometimes, frequently,* and *occasionally* come before a negative helping verb.

    He frequently doesn't do his homework.
    He sometimes doesn't do his homework.

    b. *Usually, often,* and *generally* can come before or after a negative helping verb.

    He often doesn't do his homework.
    or
    He doesn't often do his homework.

    c. *Sometimes* may also come at the beginning of a sentence.

    Sometimes he doesn't do his homework.

Here are some additional examples of the use of adverbs of frequency, showing their meanings:

100 percent of the time:	Weddings are <u>always</u> joyous occasions.
80 percent of the time:	He <u>usually</u> arrives in a white car.
	He <u>generally</u> arrives in a white car.
60 percent of the time:	They <u>often</u> provide a dowry.
	They <u>frequently</u> provide a dowry.
40 percent of the time:	He <u>sometimes</u> arrives on a white elephant.
	He <u>occasionally</u> arrives on a white elephant.
20 percent of the time:	The party <u>seldom</u> ends before midnight.
10 percent of the time:	Weddings are <u>rarely</u> held in the morning.
0 percent of the time:	The bride <u>never</u> takes off the necklace of black beads while her husband is living.

Because the last three adverbs of frequency in this list are negative in meaning, begin your answer with the word "No" if you use one to answer a question.

seldom = not often	Do you drink wine? No, I seldom drink wine.
rarely = not usually	Do you like to go to movies? No, I rarely go to movies.
never = not ever	Do you smoke? No, I never smoke.

PRACTICE:
Simple Present Tense and Adverbs of Frequency

A. Complete the paragraph with an appropriate adverb of frequency and the correct form of the verb. Choose an adverb of frequency from the list of examples on page 33.

Example: Mr. Wright <u> always works </u> from 6:30 A.M. to 7:00 P.M. six days a week.
                          all of the time/work

Mr. and Mrs. Wright are a middle-aged couple. Mr. Wright owns a

corner grocery store. Mrs. Wright is a housewife. Mr. Wright works

hard every day, so at the end of the day, he _____ very
                                            1. 60 percent of the time/be

tired. He _____ to watch television in the evenings. He
          2. every evening/like

_____ to go out at night, so Mrs. Wright _____
3. not at all/want   4. once in a while/complain

to him. She _____ to go out to dinner or visit with
            5. most of the time/like

friends. After all, she _____ at home alone during the day,
                        6. most of the time/be

so in the evenings, she _____ staying at home. This causes a
                        7. not often/enjoy

family problem, and the Wrights _____ the evening
                                8. now and then/spend

arguing. Then they are both unhappy.

B. Choose a classmate from a different country from your own and ask each other questions about traditional weddings in your countries. Ask the following questions and other questions of your own. Use the simple present tense and different adverbs of frequency in your answers.

1. When do weddings often take place in your country?

   Weddings often take place in the month of June in the United States.

2. Do weddings usually take place in the morning?

3. Do they ever take place at night?

4. Where do they usually take place? Do they ever take place anywhere else?

5. What color is the bride's dress? Is it always that color?

6. What else does the bride traditionally wear?

7. What does the groom wear?

8. Who sometimes cries at a wedding? Who rarely cries?

9. Is there a party after the wedding?

10. Where is the party usually held?

11. What happens at the party?

12. What kind of food and drinks are served?

13. Are weddings expensive in your country?

14. Who pays for weddings in your country?

15. Do the couple often or seldom pay for their own wedding?

Comma Rules

Commas are used within a sentence in the following ways:

RULES	EXAMPLES
1. To separate words, phrases, or clauses in a series (a group of three or more).	Everyone eats, drinks, dances, and has a good time at a wedding. The bride, groom, and their guests play some traditional games.
NOTE: Do **not** use a comma if there are only two items.	They paint designs on the palms of her hands and on the soles of her feet.
2. To separate the parts of dates and addresses, **except** before ZIP codes.	The Smith family lives at 3237 Atlantic Avenue, Pittsburgh, Pennsylvania 66711. They moved there on January 1, 1990.

(continued on the next page)

3. After most time order expressions.	First, the older brother brings gifts. Next, the groom arrives in a white car. Then the priest marries them. After that, they walk around the fire seven times. Finally, the groom makes seven promises. After the ceremony, there is a big party.
4. Before the coordinating conjunction in a compound sentence (that is, to separate the first simple sentence from the second simple sentence when the two are joined together by one of these words: *and, but, so, or, nor, for, yet).*	He is dressed in rich clothing, and he wears a special headdress. At first, the dye is green, but it turns red the next morning. He usually arrives in a white car, or he sometimes rides a white elephant.
NOTE: **Never** start a line with a comma, period, question mark, or exclamation mark.	**Wrong:** George left the party early , and Sam went with him. **Right:** George left the party, and Sam went with him.

PRACTICE:
Punctuation

A. Add commas, periods, question marks, and/or exclamation marks wherever they are necessary in the following sentences.

1. Daisy, Tomiko, Keiko, and Nina share an apartment near the school.

2. The address of their apartment is 3245 North Lafayette Street, Chicago, Illinois 80867.

3. Tomiko and Keiko are from Japan, and Nina and Daisy are from Venezuela.

4. Nina and Keiko have the same birthday. Both of the girls were born on June 3, 1978.

5. How old are they today?

6. All of the girls like to cook, but none of them like to wash the dishes afterward.

7. That is typical.

8. They have delicious meals. Last night they ate Japanese tempura, Venezuelan *arroz con pollo*, Chinese vegetables, and American ice cream.

9. First, Nina made the rice. Then Keiko cooked the tempura. After that, Tomiko prepared the vegetables.

10. After dinner, Daisy served the dessert.

11. They could choose chocolate or vanilla ice cream, or they could have vanilla ice cream with chocolate sauce.

(handwritten at top: have a lump in your throat?)

B. Answer the following questions with complete sentences.

1. Where were you born?

   I was born in San Juan, Puerto Rico.

2. When were you born? (Begin your answer with "I was born on . . .")

   I was born on 14.2...1961.

3. What is your address in this country?

   4180 Hamilton ... 304, San Jose, ... 12130

4. What is today's date?

   Today ... 73.03.06.

5. What are three of your favorite foods?

   Chinese food, ... and ...

6. What do you usually do on weekends? (Name at least four activities.)

   _I go ..._

7. What elementary school did you attend, and where did (do) you go to high school?

   I attended to shahrokhi ... in ...

8. What are two or three goals in your life?

   _..._

WRITING PRACTICE: *A Traditional Wedding*

Use the answers to questions 1–12 from Part B of the Practice on page 35 and write two paragraphs telling about a traditional wedding in a classmate's country.

- You might begin the first paragraph with a general sentence like this one:

  Weddings in _____ follow a traditional pattern.

  In the first paragraph, write about the answers to questions 1 through 8. Add other general information if you wish.

- You might begin the second paragraph with a sentence like this one:

  There is always a big party after the ceremony.

  In the second paragraph, write about the answers to questions 9 through 12, and add other information if you wish.

- Use time order in your paragraphs when it is appropriate.

(continued on the next page)

- Practice using adverbs of frequency and the comma rules from this chapter.
- With a partner, edit and revise your composition. Check your own and your partner's composition, especially for -*s* on third-person singular present tense verbs, for the correct position of adverbs of frequency, and for correct comma usage.

PART 3 Sentence Structure

The model for this section is a folktale. A folktale is a traditional story that had been passed down orally from one generation to the next until someone finally wrote it down. Every culture is rich in folktales. This one is from France.

MODEL:
Compound Sentences

Monsieur Seguin's Goat
as retold by Sabrina Giner

A long time ago, in the middle of the Alps lived an old man with his goat, Blanchette. She was a wonderful white goat and was very kind to her master, Monsieur Seguin. They had lived together for many years.

Blanchette was always fastened[1] to a tree. She was often sad, and sometimes she didn't eat her food. Every day, she looked at the big mountains and dreamed of being free to explore them. One day, she asked her master for more freedom. She said, "You can tie me with a longer rope, or you can build a special enclosure for me." First, he tied her with a longer rope, but Blanchette was still sad. A few days later, he built a special enclosure. At first, Blanchette was very happy about this decision, but soon the enclosure appeared very small in front of the big mountains. One summer night, Blanchette decided to leave for the mountains, so the next morning, she jumped out of the enclosure and ran away.

The fields seemed so vast[2] to her. "I am free," she said. She ate many varieties of plants, and she enjoyed meeting new friends. All day, she ran in the Alps until the sun set behind the hills.

Blanchette was surprised when the moon appeared in the sky. Then she became afraid because she remembered that the old man had told her how dangerous the night is in the mountains. She heard a strange noise, so she

---

[1]**fastened:** tied; [2]**vast:** big

decided to go back to her enclosure. She walked for a long time but couldn't
20   find the road. Finally, she became very tired, so she decided to stop. She tried
to rest, but her fear prevented her from sleeping. In the darkness, she saw a
shape. It was a wolf! They fought for a few minutes, and Blanchette's leg was
hurt. She shouted for help but nobody heard her. The wolf ate her, and the
poor old man never saw his little goat again.

25   Blanchette wanted to be free, but freedom can be dangerous when we disobey.

QUESTIONS ON THE MODEL

1. What kind of order does this folktale use?

2. Underline the time words and phrases in the narration and add any new ones to the list on page 27.

Compound Sentences with and, but, so, *and* or

A **compound sentence** is composed of two simple sentences joined together by a comma and a **coordinating conjunction.**

There are seven coordinating conjunctions in English: *and, but, so, or, for, nor,* and *yet.* In this chapter, you will learn to use the first four.

Rules for Using Coordinating Conjunctions

RULES	EXAMPLES
1. Use *and* to join sentences that are alike.	She was often sad, **and** sometimes she didn't eat her food.
2. Use *but* to join sentences that are opposite or show contrast.	At first, Blanchette was very happy about this decision, **but** soon the enclosure appeared very small in front of the big mountains.
3. Use *so* to join sentences when the second sentence expresses the result of something described in the first sentence.	One summer night, Blanchette decided to leave for the mountains, **so** the next morning, she jumped out of the enclosure and ran away.
4. Use *or* to join sentences that give choices or alternatives.	You can tie me with a longer rope, **or** you can build a special enclosure for me.
NOTE: Use a comma before the coordinating conjunction in compound sentences only. Do not use a comma when joining compound elements in simple sentences.	

Compound sentence: (comma)

Blanchette was often sad, and sometimes she didn't eat her food.

Simple sentence with a compound verb: (no comma)

Blanchette was often sad and sometimes didn't eat her food.

The comma is sometimes omitted in short compound sentences.

Short compound sentence: (comma may be omitted)

She shouted for help but nobody heard her.

PRACTICE:
Compound Sentences with and, but, so, *and* or

A. Draw a circle around all of the coordinating conjunctions in the story about Monsieur Seguin's goat. Explain why some of them have commas, but others don't. (For additional practice, do the same for the model on page 26.)

She was a wonderful white goat ⟨and⟩ was very kind to her master, Monsieur Seguin.

(This is a simple sentence—no comma.)

B. Decide which of the following are compound sentences and which are simple sentences. Write CS or SS in the space at the left. Then add commas to the compound sentences.

Omusubi Kororin
A Japanese Folktale
as retold by Masako Inoue

_SS_ **1.** Once upon a time, an old couple lived in the countryside.

_____ **2.** One day, the old man went to work in the forest and took his usual lunch of three rice balls.

_____ **3.** During his lunch, he dropped a rice ball and it rolled into a hole in the ground.

_____ **4.** He heard happy singing coming from the hole so he dropped the other two rice balls into it.

_____ **5.** A little mouse came out of the hole and invited him in.

_____ **6.** Inside the hole, some mice were having a party and one of them said to him, "Thank you for the delicious rice balls."

_____ **7.** They invited him to join them so he did.

_____ **8.** After a while, the mice told him to choose a box as a reward for his generosity.[1]

_____ **9.** He could choose a big box or he could choose a small box.

---

[1]**generosity:** willingness to give

C. For each set of sentences below, make a compound sentence or a simple sentence with a compound complement. Use the coordinating conjunction *and, but, or,* or *so* to join the sentences. Punctuate carefully.

Omusubi Kororin *(continued)*

10. He thought about taking a big box. He finally chose a small one.

11. He went home. He and his wife opened the box.

12. The box was full of gold coins. They were very surprised and pleased.

13. A greedy[2] neighbor heard about their good fortune. He quickly made plans to visit the same hole.

14. He pushed a lot of rice balls down the hole. The mice invited him in.

15. The man was very, very greedy. He wanted all of the boxes.

16. He pretended to be a cat. The mice became frightened. They ran away. (Connect all three sentences.)

17. The greedy man was left alone in the dark hole. He had to try to dig his way out of the hole.

18. He dug a tunnel all the way to his house. He couldn't carry any boxes with him. He got nothing. (Connect all three sentences.)

D. Write compound sentences using the coordinating conjunctions you have learned. Follow the directions given.

1. Write a sentence that tells one thing you like to do and one thing you don't like to do. (Use *but*.)

Example: I like to swim, but I don't like to play tennis.

2. Write a sentence that tells two things you do every morning after you get up. (Use *and*.)

3. Write a sentence that tells two things you *might* do during your next vacation. (Use *or*.)

4. Write a sentence that tells the results of the following. Begin each sentence with "I am/was . . ." (Use *so* in all three sentences.)

 a. being born in (your country)

 Example: I was born in France, so I speak French.

 b. being the oldest child/youngest/middle/only in your family

 c. being a lazy/hard-working student

5. Write a sentence that tells two different careers you *might* have in the future. (Use *or*.)

---

[2]**greedy:** wanting to have more than you need or have earned

Sentence Combining

Most of the sentences in the following exercise are simple sentences. When a writer uses only short, simple sentences like these, his or her writing seems choppy and immature. This kind of writing can be improved by combining short sentences to make compound sentences or simple sentences with compound verbs. To do this exercise, work with a partner and proceed as follows:

1. Combine the sentences beside each number to make one sentence. Your new sentences may be compound, or they may be simple with a compound verb. Use coordinating conjunctions that fit the meaning, and punctuate carefully. If there is only one sentence, simply copy the sentence without changing it. The first three have been done for you.

2. Write the sentences as a connected story. Divide it into three paragraphs using time order. What time divisions can you use? Where can each new paragraph begin? (Hint: Look for time phrases.)

3. Finally, finish the story on your own. Write the fourth paragraph and tell about two or three more misfortunes that happen to Lily after she arrived home. Write both compound sentences and simple sentences with compound verbs.

4. You may write the story on the lines provided on page 43 or on a separate piece of paper. Don't forget to indent each paragraph!

Lily's Terrible Day

1. Lily had a terrible day today.

2. She woke up late. She had to hurry.

3. She was hungry. She didn't have time to eat any breakfast.

4. She got dressed. She grabbed her books. She ran all the way to the bus stop.

5. The bus was just leaving. She yelled. The bus driver didn't hear her.

6. She could take a taxi to school. She could walk.

7. She decided to walk.

8. One hour later, she arrived at school.

9. She had missed her first class. She was late to her second one.

10. She hadn't studied for her calculus test. Of course, she didn't do well on it.

11. Her biology teacher told her she had to repeat three labs. She would fail the course.

12. After school, she walked to the bus stop.

13. She hadn't brought her umbrella. She got very wet.

14. The bus finally came. She got on.

15. She reached into her pocket for bus fare. Her pocket was empty.

16. Her money was gone!

17. She couldn't pay the bus fare. She had to walk home in the rain.

Lily's Terrible Day

Lily had a terrible day today. She woke up late, so she had to hurry. She was hungry, but she didn't have time to eat any breakfast.

_____

_____

_____

_____

_____

_____

At last she got home. She _____

_____

_____ . Some days she wished she had stayed in bed.

PART **4** The Writing Process

On Your Own!

Now let's complete the writing process you began at the beginning of the unit. Write a composition of one or more paragraphs about a memorable event or a memorable experience in your life. Follow these steps in order to write a good composition:

STEP 1:
Prewrite to Get Ideas

This was the freewriting you did at the beginning of this unit.

STEP 2:
Organize the Ideas

Put the events into time order: make a list of the events or number them on your freewriting paper. Use this list to guide you as you write.

STEP 3:
Write the Rough Draft

Write ROUGH DRAFT at the top of your paper.

- Begin your composition with a sentence that tells what event or experience you are going to write about.

  I'll never forget my wedding day.

  The most memorable vacation I ever took was a bicycle trip across Canada.

- Use time order to organize your composition. Use time order words and phrases.

- Pay attention to your sentence structure. Write both simple and compound sentences, and punctuate them correctly.

STEP 4:
Edit the Rough Draft

First, use the Editing Checklist and edit your paragraph by answering the Writer's Questions. Then ask a classmate, the peer editor, to read your paragraph and complete the Peer Editor's Answers and Comments section of the checklist. The peer editor should suggest ways to improve your composition.

EDITING CHECKLIST

Writer's Questions	Peer Editor's Answers and Comments
FORMAT	
1. Is the format correct?	Check the title, indenting, margins, and double spacing.
ORGANIZATION	
2. Does the composition use time order?	yes no
3. Are there time order words and phrases to show time order?	Write the time order words and phrases used:
4. If the composition has more than one paragraph, are the paragraphs divided logically? Does the first sentence of each paragraph tell the reader what the paragraph is about?	How many paragraphs are there? What is the topic of each paragraph?
5. Does the composition end with a concluding sentence?	Copy the concluding sentence here:
GRAMMAR AND MECHANICS	
6. Is there a period at the end of each sentence?	Check each sentence. Does each one end with a period? yes no Add any missing periods.
7. Are capital letters used where necessary?	Write down any words that should be capitalized and are not:
8. Are the verb tenses correct?	What verb tense is used most frequently? Are any other verb tenses used? yes no
9. Are commas used correctly?	Check each sentence for commas. Especially check any commas used with coordinating conjunctions *(and, but, so, or)* to make sure the commas are necessary.
SENTENCE STRUCTURE	
10. Does each sentence contain at least one subject and one verb and express a complete thought?	Underline any sentences that you have doubts about.
11. Does the composition contain both simple and compound sentences?	Count the simple sentences: Count the compound sentences:
12. Are the compound sentences punctuated correctly?	Circle coordinating conjunctions and double-check the commas.

STEP 5:
Write the Second Draft

Write SECOND DRAFT at the top of your paper. Write the second draft of your composition to hand in to your instructor.

STEP 6:
Write the Final Draft

After your instructor returns your composition, write a neat final copy to hand in for final evaluation. Write FINAL DRAFT at the top of your paper.

ADDITIONAL WRITING

1. Write about a holiday or special festival in your country. Use time order. Write about the preparations for the holiday and then about the actual celebration itself.

2. Write a folktale that you remember from your country.

Unit # 3 Description

PREWRITING
- *Clustering*

ORGANIZATION
- *Description*
- *Spatial Order*
   Spatial Order Words and Phrases

GRAMMAR AND MECHANICS
- *Present Continuous Tense*
- *The Subject* it
- *The Expletive* there
   Subject-Verb Agreement Rules

SENTENCE STRUCTURE
- *Compound Sentences with* yet, for, *and* nor
   Rules for Using Coordinating Conjunctions
- *Position of Prepositional Phrases*

THE WRITING PROCESS

*I*n the previous unit, you learned about writing narration. In this unit, you will focus on writing description. Narration is writing about events that happen and uses time order. **Description** is writing about how something (or someone) looks and uses space order.

Prewriting: Clustering

Clustering is a prewriting technique used by writers to produce ideas. When you cluster, you start by writing your topic in a circle in the middle of your paper. As you think of related ideas, you write these ideas in smaller circles around the first circle. The related idea in each small circle may produce even more ideas, and therefore more circles, around it. When you have run out of ideas, your paper might look something like the following model:

MODEL:
Clustering

CLUSTERING TOPIC: A PLACE FROM MY CHILDHOOD

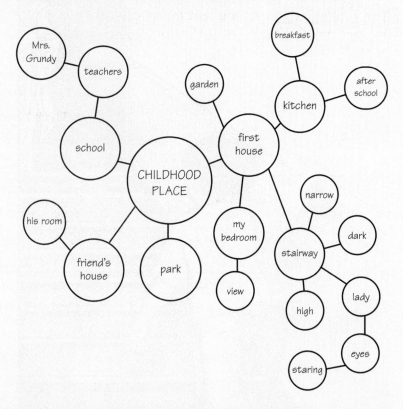

You can see that this writer had the most ideas about the first house he lived in as a child. When he thought more about his house, he remembered a stairway in the house and a mysterious lady at the top of it. Because of the richness of his ideas about the stairway, which you can see from the large number of circles, he chose it as the topic of his paragraph. His final paragraph is on pages 49–50.

ACTIVITY

A. Practice the clustering technique. Choose one of the topics from the list below, and write it in a large circle in the center of a piece of paper. Think about the topic for one or two minutes. Then write each new idea that comes into your mind in smaller circles around the large circle. Next, think about the idea in each smaller circle for one or two minutes. Write any new ideas in even smaller circles. You should spend about twenty minutes on this exercise.

TOPICS

A place from my childhood   The view from my window
An old person I know   A place that is special to me

B. After you have finished, tell a classmate about your topic. Save your clustering paper. You will use it later to write a paragraph.

MODEL PARAGRAPH:

Description

As you read the model paragraph, notice how the description moves from the bottom of the stairway to the top.

The Stairway

by Toshiki Yamazaki

When I was two or three years old, I lived in a house that had a strange atmosphere.[1] I do not remember anything about the house except the stairway. It was dark, squeaking, and quite narrow, and its steps were a little high for me to climb up. From the bottom of the stairway, it seemed like an

5   endless climb to the top. Beyond the darkness at the top of the stairway, there was a middle-aged, elegant lady leaning against the wall. I had to pass her every time I went to my room, for my room was the first room from the stairs on the second floor. The lady wore a beautiful dress with a quiet pattern and a tinge[2] of blue, and her peaceful eyes stared at me every time I went up the

10   stairs. As I carefully climbed up the last step, her eyes became fixed[3] on me. I was scared, yet I was also curious about the lady. She didn't talk, nor did she move. She just stood there and watched me clamber[4] up the stairs. One day I touched her, but she did not react. Her face did not change expression, nor did she even blink. She just kept staring at me with her glittering[5] eyes. Later, we

15   moved out of the house, and I never saw her again. Now I know that the lady

---

[1]**atmosphere:** mood of a place; [2]**tinge:** small amount; [3]**fixed:** not moving; [4]**clamber:** climb with difficulty; [5]**glittering:** shining, sparkling

was a mannequin.[6] My aunt, whom I lived with, used it for her dressmaking class. I did not know my mother. Maybe I imagined that the mannequin standing at the top of the stairs was my mother. The stairway with the strange atmosphere has an important place in my earliest memories.

QUESTIONS ON THE MODEL

1. What does the writer say about the atmosphere of the house in the first sentence?

2. How does the writer describe the stairway? Underline the words that describe it.

3. When he first describes the woman, is he looking up at her or down at her? What does he describe about her first? What does he describe last?

4. Which of the senses does the writer of this paragraph appeal to in his description: sight, smell, sound, touch, and/or taste?

PART 1 Organization

Description

Descriptive writing appeals to the senses, so it tells how something looks, feels, smells, tastes, and/or sounds. A good description is like a "word picture"; the reader can imagine the object, place, or person in his or her mind. A writer of a good description is like an artist who paints a picture that can be "seen" clearly in the mind of the reader.

Spatial Order

Just as an artist plans where to place each object in a painting, a writer plans where to put each object in a "word painting." In a description, writers often use **spatial order** to organize their ideas. Spatial order is the arrangement of items in order by space.

For example, when describing your favorite room at home, you could first describe things on the left side of the doorway and then move clockwise around to the right side. You could also start on the right and move counterclockwise around to the left. If you jumped back and forth, it would be very difficult for the reader to try to see the room in his or her mind.

When you describe a person, you could begin with an overall impression and then focus on the person's head, then the face, and then on one part of the face such as the eyes. It does not usually matter whether the spatial organization is

---

[6]**mannequin:** life-size model of a human used for displaying clothes

left to right, right to left, near to far, far to near, outside to inside, inside to outside, top to bottom, or bottom to top. It is only helpful to use some kind of spatial order when you write a description.

The model paragraph "The Stairway" uses spatial organization. In describing the stairway, the writer shows that as a little boy, his first view was from the bottom looking up at the mannequin. Then he climbed up the stairway until he reached the top. Thus, the spatial organization is from bottom to top. When he describes the mannequin, he first gives an overall impression (the way she was leaning against the wall and what her dress looked like). Then he focuses on her face and finally on her unblinking eyes. Thus, the spatial organization is from far to near.

PRACTICE:
Spatial Order

A. Study the map of Greenhills College, a small private college in the United States. Pretend that you have to describe the campus to a visitor who is not familiar with the campus. Discuss with a partner or a small group three different ways (back to front, right to left, etc.) to organize your description using spatial organization.

1. _____

2. _____

3. _____

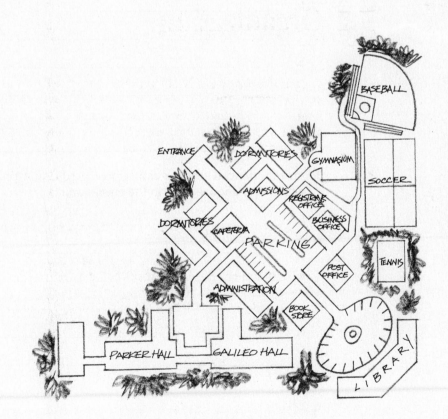

B. Each of the following sentences could be the first sentence of a descriptive paragraph. First, discuss with your partner or group some possible details that describe the place. Next, decide on the best kind of spatial order to use in the description: right to left, left to right, top to bottom, far to near, outside to inside, etc. Finally, write your details on the lines below in spatial order.

1. After my sister has spent two hours getting ready for a date, her room looks as if it has been hit by a magnitude 8.5 earthquake.

   a. From the doorway, you see nothing but a mountain of clothes all over the floor.

   b. _____

   _____

   c. _____

   _____

   d. _____

2. The park near my house is full of activity on a sunny weekend afternoon.

   a. _____

   _____

   b. _____

   _____

   c. _____

   _____

   d. _____

   _____

3. An experienced teacher can almost predict the final grade of students by where they choose to sit in the classroom.

   a. _____

   _____

   b. _____

   _____

   c. _____

   _____

   d. _____

   _____

Spatial Order Words and Phrases

Just as there are words and phrases to show time order, there are words and phrases to show spatial organization. They are often prepositional phrases of location or position. Some spatial order expressions are

at the top of	next to	inside
in the center	between	across from
on the left	behind	_____
in front of	in back of	_____
in the front of	in the back of	_____
on the trail	_____	_____
into	_____	_____
_____	_____	_____

PRACTICE:
Spatial Order Words and Phrases

A. Find and underline the spatial order words and phrases used in the model paragraph "The Stairway," on pages 49–50. Add them to the list above.

B. Look again at the map of Greenhills College on page 51. Working with a partner, take turns telling each other the location of the places in the following list. Use spatial order expressions in your sentences.

Example: The administration building is across from the parking lot.

the administration building	the business office	the post office
Parker Hall (classrooms)	the admissions office	the entrance gate
the bookstore	Galileo Hall (classrooms)	the baseball field
the dormitories	the parking lot	the library
the registrar's office	tennis courts	the soccer field
	the gymnasium	the student cafeteria

WRITING PRACTICE:

Spatial Order

Write a one-paragraph description of the campus of Greenhills College to a friend in your country. Be sure to include some descriptive details.

- You might begin your paragraph with a sentence like this one:

  or The campus of Greenhills College is very compact.
  The campus of Greenhills College is shaped like an arrow.

- Use spatial order in your description. Use spatial order expressions.

- Use your imagination and include some details that appeal to the senses. Try to "paint a picture in words."

- With a partner, edit and revise your paragraph. Check your own and your partner's paragraphs especially for spatial organization, spatial order expressions, and vivid descriptive details.

PART 2 Grammar and Mechanics

As you read the model essay below, notice the verb tenses. Notice also how the expressions *it is, there is,* and *there are* are used.

Havasu Canyon

There is a canyon[1] in Northern Arizona that is the most beautiful spot on Earth. It is called Havasu Canyon, and it is part of the Havasupai Indian reservation.[2] It is not easy to get there, for it is ten or fifteen miles from the nearest road. You have to hike down a long, hot trail, or you can hire a Havasupai

5   guide to take you there on horseback. The trip takes all day. On the trail down into the canyon, you see only rock, sand, and an occasional lizard.[3] It is very dry, for this is desert country. There is no water on the trail, nor is there any shade. After eight miles or so, you begin to notice a few green plants growing here and there, and after another mile or two, you come to a creek.[4] The water from this creek

10 completely changes the landscape. There are trees and green grass, and it is cooler.

At the end of the trail, you arrive at Havasupai village. It is a quiet place. Dogs are sleeping in the streets, and the villagers are standing in the doorways of their small homes silently watching you, a stranger, pass by. They aren't smiling, yet they don't seem unfriendly.

15 Beyond the village, a trail leads to the top of a steep cliff[5] overlooking Havasu Canyon. Your first view of the canyon takes your breath away.[6] Directly in front of you, the trail disappears straight down the two hundred-foot cliff. There are deep steps cut into the rock, and there is a strong chain bolted[7] to the cliff. You have to hold the chain when you climb down, or you might fall. On your right,

20 you see a beautiful waterfall. Water is falling straight down into a bright blue-green pool below. Directly across the canyon, hundreds of small waterfalls are gushing[8] from the cliff face, and little green ferns[9] are growing everywhere.

---

[1]**canyon:** narrow valley with steep walls, cut into the earth by running water; [2]**reservation:** area of land where Native Americans (Indians) live; [3]**lizard:** reptile that lives in dry areas; [4]**creek:** small river; [5]**cliff:** high, steep wall of rock; [6]**takes your breath away:** makes you unable to speak (from pleasure); [7]**bolted:** fastened with a bolt (a screw with no point); [8]**gushing:** coming out very fast in large amounts; [9]**fern:** type of plant with leaves like feathers

Below, the water in the pool is cascading[10] from one bright turquoise[11] pool into another until it disappears into the trees on the left. As you view this scene, you can only think that Havasu Canyon is truly a magical place.

25

QUESTIONS ON THE MODEL

1. What kind of spatial organization does the writer use in the first and second paragraphs? In the third paragraph?

2. What verb tense occurs for the first time in the second paragraph and again in the second half of the third paragraph? Why is this verb tense used in these places?

3. Underline the spatial order expressions if you haven't already done so. Add any new ones to the list of spatial order expressions on page 53.

Present Continuous Tense

The **present continuous tense** is used to describe actions that are actually taking place at the present time and are temporary.

The sun is shining. (at this moment, temporarily)
The newlyweds are living with her parents. (at the present time, temporarily)
She's smoking. (She's smoking a cigarette at this moment.)

Compare the meaning of the sentences above with the meaning of these sentences with verbs in the simple present tense:

The sun shines 360 days a year in Miami. (habitual action, every day)
The newlyweds live with her parents. (permanently)
She smokes. (It's her habit.)

Remember that the present continuous tense is not possible with certain verbs. These verbs include

1. verbs of emotional states: *admire, dislike, envy, hate, like, love*

2. verbs of mental states: *believe, doubt, forget, know, need, prefer, remember, think, understand, want, wonder*

3. verbs of the senses: *feel, hear, see, smell, taste*

4. verbs of existing states: *appear, be, exist, look like, seem*

The present continuous tense is frequently used in writing descriptions. When you want to tell about the activities that are happening in the scene you are describing, use the present continuous tense.

---

[10]**cascading:** falling in waves; [11]**turquoise:** blue-green

A. Underline the present continuous verbs in the description of Havasu Canyon on pages 54–55.

B. Complete the essay with the present continuous or simple present tense of the verb.

My Banana Garden

by Quang Nguyen

Behind my house, there ___is___ a large piece of land that is
      1. be

surrounded by banana trees. This place _____ very wild and
      2. be

disorderly. Crowds of banana trees _____ freely everywhere.
      3. grow

Their green leaves _____ so thick that sunlight cannot pass
      4. be

through. The ground underneath the trees _____ so moist that
      5. be

wild mushrooms and plants _____ all year around. In the center
      6. grow

_____ a wild field where the children of my village often
7. be

_____ kites.
8. fly

Every evening, just before the sun _____, some birds
      9. set

_____ to look for a place to rest their tired wings. They _____
10. arrive   11. want

to land in the dark banana garden, but the banana leaves _____ too
      12. be

wide to be made into nests. The birds _____ out and _____
      13. cry   14. fly

away, seeking a better place to nest. During the rainy season, it

_____ for days and days, and the rain _____ the banana
15. rain   16. make

garden produce a very strange melody. Whenever I _____ bored, I
      17. be

_____ near my window and _____ to this wonderful song.
18. sit   19. listen

Right now, I _____ at my window watching the children fly
      20. sit

kites in the meadow. The children's colorful kites _____ happily
      21. fly

in the wide open sky, but the wind _____ stronger, and it
      22. become

_____ the children's kites toward the banana trees. The air
23. blow

_____ heavy—a sure sign of rain. Now the sky _____, and
24. feel   25. darken

it _____ to sprinkle. The children _____ into the banana
   26. start   27. run

garden and _____ under the thick leaves to keep from getting
              28. hide

wet. They _____ the rain to end quickly so that they can
       29. want

continue flying their kites. I _____ a beautiful rainbow in the
                 30. see

distance, so I _____ the rain will stop soon.
        31. know

The Subject it

> It is used in statements about weather, time, distance, and identification. *It* is the subject of the sentence but doesn't have any real meaning.

Weather:

It is very dry, for this is desert country.
It rains in the summer.
It clears up by noon.

Time:

It is Sunday.
It is three o'clock.

Distance:

It is ten or fifteen miles from the nearest road.
It is an hour's drive to the beach from my house.

Identification:

Who is it? (on the telephone or at the door)
It's Mary.
It's my cousin.

CAUTION: Do not confuse *it's* (it + is) with the possessive pronoun *its*, which has no apostrophe.

It's hot today.
The book lost its cover.

The Expletive there

> The expressions ***there is*** and ***there are*** are used in English to state that something exists.

There is a God.
There are several possible answers to that question.

Many sentences beginning with *there is* or *there are* contain expressions of place.

There are deep steps cut into the rock.
There is a strong chain bolted to the cliff.

There can begin a sentence, but it is not the subject of the sentence. *There,* like *it,* has no meaning. The real subject of the sentence comes after *is* or *are,* and the verb must agree with the real subject.

Subject-Verb Agreement Rules

RULES | **EXAMPLES**

1. If the real subject is singular or uncountable, the verb is singular. | There is a canyon in Northern Arizona that is the most beautiful spot on Earth. There is no water on the trail.

2. If the real subject is plural, the verb is plural. | There aren't any snakes in Hawaii.

3. If there are both plural and singular or uncountable subjects, the verb agrees with the subject nearest to the verb. | There is one desk and two chairs in my office.

CAUTION: Do not use *there is* and *there are* too often in the same paragraph. Overusing these expressions makes your writing uninteresting. If you notice that your paragraphs contain a lot of *there is/there are* sentences, rewrite some of them to get rid of *there is/there are.* | There is someone at the front door. Rewritten: Someone is at the front door. There are two cats fighting in the street. Rewritten: Two cats are fighting in the street.

PRACTICE:
it is, there is, there are

Complete the answers with *it is, there is,* or *there are.*

Example: How is the weather today?

_____It is_____ cold and still tonight.

_____There is_____ no wind.

1. Would you like to go sailing today? Yes, I would. _____ warm and sunny, and _____ a light breeze blowing over the water.

2. Do you have a lot of brothers and sisters? Yes, _____ twelve children in my family.

3. Where can I buy a guidebook to this city? _____ a bookstore just around the corner in the next block.

4. Who's on the phone? _____ my friend Stephanie.

5. Where is your office? _____ about a half hour's drive from my house.

6. May I have another cup of coffee, please? I'm sorry. _____ any coffee left. We drank it all. (Use a negative verb.)

7. Why is the dog barking? _____ someone at the front door.

8. Would you like to have another drink? No, thank you. _____ past midnight, and I'm a little tired. I'd like to go home.

WRITING PRACTICE: *Describing a Busy Scene*

Write a paragraph describing a busy scene, such as an airport terminal, the emergency room of a hospital, the school cafeteria at lunchtime, the scene of an automobile accident, or a sunny day at the beach.

- Begin with a sentence that names the scene you will describe and gives a general impression of it, such as the following:

   The airport terminal is full of people in a hurry.

- Use spatial order in your description.

- Use present continuous verbs where appropriate.

- Use some *there is/there are* sentences where they are appropriate, but do not use too many.

- With a partner, edit and revise your paragraph. Check your own and your partner's paragraphs especially for the correct use of present continuous tense and *there is/there are* expressions.

PART 3 Sentence Structure

Compound Sentences with yet, for, and nor

You remember from the last unit that a compound sentence is composed of two simple sentences joined together by a comma and a coordinating conjunction. There are seven coordinating conjunctions in English. In the last unit, you practiced using *and, but, or,* and *so*. In this unit, you will learn to use the other three: *yet, for,* and *nor.*

Rules for Using Coordinating Conjunctions

RULES

EXAMPLES

I. *yet* has approximately the same meaning as *but;* that is, it shows contrast or joins opposites. Use *yet* when the second part of the sentence says something unexpected or surprising.

They aren't smiling, **yet** they don't seem unfriendly.
I was scared, **yet** I was also curious about the old lady.

2. *for* has the same meaning as *because;* use *for* to introduce a reason or cause.

It is not easy to get there, **for** it is ten or fifteen miles from the nearest road.
I had to pass her every time I went to my room, **for** my room was the first room from the stairs on the second floor.

3. *nor* means "not this and not that"; use *nor* to join two negative sentences.

NOTE: The word order after *nor* is like a question. The helping verb (*is, does, did, can, will,* etc.) comes before the subject of the part of the sentence introduced by *nor.*

There is no water on the trail, **nor** is there any shade.
(There isn't any water. There isn't any shade.)

She didn't talk, **nor** did she move.
(She didn't talk. She didn't move.)

PRACTICE:
Compound Sentences with yet, for, *and* nor

A. Join the two sentences in each of the following pairs by using a comma and one of these coordinating conjunctions: *yet, for, nor.*

1. Moslems don't drink alcohol. They don't eat pork.

2. Christians are not supposed to work on Sunday. Sunday is their day to worship God.

3. People who believe in the Hindu religion do not eat beef. They believe that cows are sacred.

4. Moslem men are permitted to have four wives. Few of them have more than one.

5. Buddhist monks do not marry. They do not own property.

B. Make compound sentences from the following incomplete sentences by adding to each a simple sentence that fits the meaning.

1. I have studied English in school for six years, yet _____

   _____ .

2. Many children who watch television all day long don't learn how to read

   well, for _____ .

3. In some countries, women cannot vote, nor _____

_____

_____ .

4. The United States is one of the richest countries in the world, yet _____

_____ .

5. Everyone should learn about computers, for _____

_____ .

c. For additional practice, write two more compound sentences of your own using *nor.*

1. _____

_____

2. _____

_____

Position of Prepositional Phrases

As you learned in Unit 1, a prepositional phrase consists of a preposition and a pronoun, noun, or noun phrase. The following prepositional phrases express time, place, and possession, among other things.

Time	in the early morning
	at three o'clock
	during dinner
	after the accident
Place	in the hall
	beyond the darkness
	in front of the house
	at the top of the stairs
Possession	the color *of the house*
	the top *of the stairway*
	a girl *with red hair*

Prepositional phrases are often moveable. Some (but not all) prepositional phrases can come at the beginning as well as at the end of a sentence. At the beginning of sentences, they often function as time order and spatial order signals. Moving prepositional phrases to the beginning of some sentences also adds interest and variety to your sentences. When you use time order or spatial order in a paragraph, move some prepositional phrases to the beginning of their sentences, and put a comma after them.

> or
> I was afraid of many things during my childhood.
> During my childhood, I was afraid of many things.

> or
> You arrive at Havasupai Village at the end of the trail.
> At the end of the trail, you arrive at Havasupai village.

> or
> A trail beyond the village leads to the top of a steep cliff overlooking Havasu Canyon.
> Beyond the village, a trail leads to the top of a steep cliff overlooking Havasu Canyon.

Not all prepositional phrases can be moved:

> The color of the house was white.
> **Not Possible** Of the house, the color was white.

> He married a girl with red hair.
> **Not Possible** With red hair, he married a girl.

PRACTICE:
Moving Prepositional Phrases

Work with a partner on this exercise if you wish to.

1. Underline all of the prepositional phrases in the following sentences.

2. Rewrite each sentence by moving an appropriate prepositional phrase to the beginning of its sentence. In some sentences, two prepositional phrases must be moved together. Punctuate your new sentences correctly.

> **Example:** Two tropical storms raced <u>through the Caribbean Sea</u> <u>in the fall of 1995.</u>
> In the fall of 1995, two tropical storms raced through the Caribbean Sea.

1. Huge trees fell, blocking streets, damaging buildings, and knocking out power during the storms.

_____

_____

2. Seventy-five-mile-an-hour winds ripped steel roofs off some homes on Saint Croix.

_____

_____

3. Twelve-foot waves flooded homes and businesses in the towns near the coast.

_____

_____

4. The giant storms also damaged banana plantations and sugarcane fields in the eastern Caribbean.

_____

_____

5. Scientists have gathered useful information about hurricanes from these two storms.

_____

_____

WRITING PRACTICE: *Sentence Combining*

Work with a partner on this sentence-combining exercise.

1. Combine the sentences in each group into one sentence. Some of your new sentences will be simple, and some will be compound.

2. Then write the sentences as a connected paragraph. The result will be a description of the apartment in the drawing.

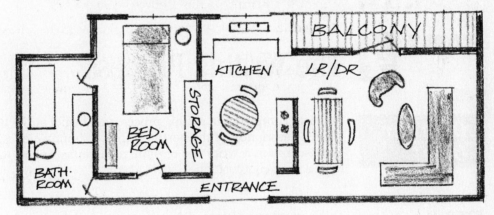

My Apartment

1. My apartment is very small.
It is quite comfortable.

2. It has a living room.
It has a kitchen.
It has a bedroom.
It has a bathroom.

3. There is something on the left side of the entrance.
There are doors.
There are two of them.

4. One door leads to the bathroom.
The other door leads to the bedroom.

(continued on the next page)

5. The bathroom is on the far left.
   The bedroom is next to the bathroom.

6. Directly in front of the entrance is something.
   It is the kitchen.

7. There is something between the bedroom and the kitchen.
   It is a large storage closet.

8. On the right side of the entrance is something.
   It is the living room.

9. The living room is quite large.
   It also serves as a dining room.

10. In the back wall of the living room, there is something.
    There is a door.
    A door leads somewhere.
    A door leads to a narrow balcony.

11. In nice weather, you can do something.
    You can sit outside.
    You can enjoy the view.

PART 4 The Writing Process

Now let's complete the writing process you began at the beginning of the unit. Write a description of the person or place about which you did the clustering exercise. You may write one or more paragraphs. Follow these steps in order to write a good composition.

STEP 1:
Prewrite to Get Ideas

This is the clustering you did at the beginning of this unit.

STEP 2:
Organize the Ideas

Decide what kind of spatial order will work the best for your description: left to right, far to near, etc.

STEP 3:
Write the Rough Draft

Write ROUGH DRAFT at the top of your paper.

- You might begin your paragraph with a sentence that tells what person or place you are going to write about and gives a general impression.

  The corner of the library where I study is my favorite place.

  The neighbor's son frightened everyone in my class at school.

- Take care to use the correct verb tenses. Use the present continuous tense if it is appropriate to describe activities.
- Pay attention to your sentence structure. Use *there is/there are* sentences if they are appropriate. Use a combination of simple and compound sentences.
- Begin some of your sentences with prepositional phrases of place to show the spatial organization.

STEP 4:
Edit the Rough Draft

Edit the rough draft. Follow the editing procedure you used in previous units.

EDITING CHECKLIST

Writer's Questions	Peer Editor's Answers and Comments
FORMAT	
1. Is the format correct?	Check the title, indenting, margins, and double spacing.
ORGANIZATION	
2. Does the composition use spatial order?	Write the kind of spatial order (left to right, right to left, etc.):
3. Are there spatial order expressions to show the order?	List the spatial order expressions used:
4. Do the descriptive details appeal to the senses?	Which senses does the description appeal to? Circle one or more words: sight sound touch taste smell
GRAMMAR AND MECHANICS	
5. Is there a period at the end of each sentence?	Check each sentence: Does each one end with a period? yes no Add missing periods.
6. Are capital letters used where necessary?	Write down any words that should be capitalized and are not:
7. Are commas used correctly?	Circle any comma errors. Add missing commas.
8. Is present continuous tense used appropriately?	Underline the present continuous verbs. Check the subject-verb agreement of each.
9. Do any sentences begin with *there is/there are*?	Find any *there is/there are* sentences. Do the verbs agree with the real subjects? Write the part of each sentence that contains the word *there*, the verb, and the real subject:

SENTENCE STRUCTURE	
10. Does each sentence contain at least one subject and one verb and express a complete thought?	Underline any sentences that you have doubts about.
11. Does the composition contain both simple and compound sentences?	Count the simple sentences: Count the compound sentences:
12. Are the compound sentences punctuated correctly?	Circle coordinating conjunctions and double-check the commas.
13. Do some sentences begin with prepositional phrases?	How many sentences begin with a prepositional phrase? Are they followed by a comma? yes no

STEP 5:
Write the Second Draft

Write SECOND DRAFT at the top of your paper. Write the second draft of your paragraph to hand in to your instructor.

STEP 6:
Write the Final Draft

After your instructor returns your composition, write a neat final copy to hand in for final evaluation. Write FINAL DRAFT at the top of your paper.

ADDITIONAL WRITING

1. Describe a favorite painting from an art book or an interesting picture from a magazine or newspaper.

2. Describe your living space, first orally with a partner and then in writing.

   a. Make a simple drawing of the place where you are presently living. This could be your bedroom, apartment, or house. Use the drawing of the apartment on page 63 as an example. Do not show your sketch to your partner.

   b. With your partner, take turns describing your home to each other. Use spatial order to organize your description. Your partner will try to draw your home from your description. He or she can ask questions like the following to help clarify points:

   Is the kitchen to the right or to the left of the dining room? Is there a door between the bedroom and the bathroom?

   c. Finally, write your description in a well-organized paragraph. Begin with a sentence like one of these:

   My apartment is small and efficient.
   My bedroom is bright and cheerful.
   My house isn't big, but it is large enough for our family.

Unit 4 Paragraph Organization

PREWRITING
- *Brainstorming*

ORGANIZATION
- *The Parts of a Paragraph*
    The Topic Sentence

    Supporting Sentences

    The Concluding Sentence

    The Concluding Comment

PREWRITING (continued)
- *Outlining a Paragraph*
- *Using an Outline*

THE WRITING PROCESS

*Y*ou have already been reading and perhaps writing compositions with more than one paragraph in order to increase your writing fluency. In this unit, you will study the paragraph structure in detail. You will also begin your study of expository writing. Descriptive and narrative writing, which you learned about in the first three units, are used to describe things and tell about events. **Expository** writing is used to *explain* things.

Prewriting: Brainstorming

Brainstorming is a prewriting activity in which you come up with a list of ideas about a topic on your own or in small groups with your classmates. You quickly write down a list of ideas that come to your mind as you are thinking about a general subject or a specific topic. Follow these brainstorming steps:

1. Write down your general subject or specific topic.

2. Make a list of everything that comes to your mind about it.

3. Use words, phrases, and/or sentences. Don't worry about the order of ideas, mechanics, grammar, or spelling.

4. Just keep writing down whatever comes to your mind until you run out of ideas. Because you are only brainstorming, don't be concerned if you repeat several ideas.

In the following model, the writer already had a sport in mind, so he brainstormed for ideas to develop the topic.

MODEL:
Brainstorming

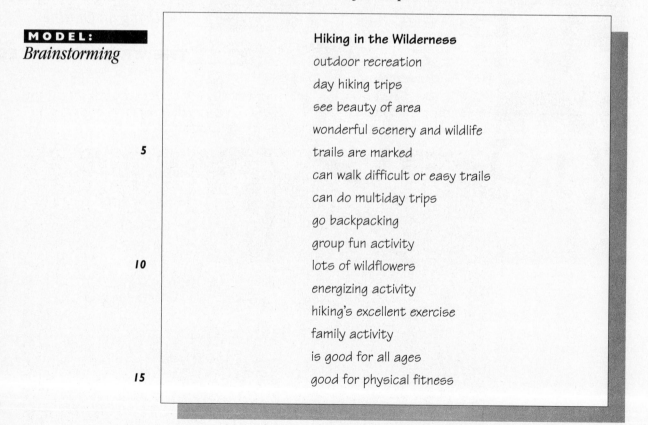

Hiking in the Wilderness

outdoor recreation

day hiking trips

see beauty of area

wonderful scenery and wildlife

5   trails are marked

can walk difficult or easy trails

can do multiday trips

go backpacking

group fun activity

10   lots of wildflowers

energizing activity

hiking's excellent exercise

family activity

is good for all ages

15   good for physical fitness

ACTIVITY

A. Choose a sport or activity that you are interested in. You can choose something you do now, have participated in in the past, or want to enjoy in the future. You might choose a sport such as swimming, tennis, volleyball, jogging, or soccer. An activity you enjoy might be dancing, playing a musical instrument, singing, acting, or playing chess.

B. Brainstorm and list as many facts as you can about your sport or activity. Read the following questions to help you get ideas for your brainstorming list.

   1. What is the sport or activity?

   2. How would you describe it?

   3. Where do you play this sport or do this activity?

   4. How many people are needed?

   5. What kind of equipment is necessary?

   6. When did you take it up?

   7. How often do you do this sport or activity?

   8. How does this activity excite you mentally and affect you physically?

   9. Why would you recommend this sport or activity to someone?

C. After you complete your brainstorming list, read through it, and draw a line through the items that you will not use.

D. Then work with a partner or a small group. Discuss your choice, using your list only as a guide. Your classmate(s) should ask you questions and share information. Take notes about anything new.

E. Save your list and notes. You will use them later to write a paragraph.

MODEL PARAGRAPH:

Paragraph Structure

As you read the model paragraph, notice how the first sentence introduces the topic: the requirements for river rafting. Also, notice that all of the sentences that follow support the topic by explaining those requirements.

River Rafting

River rafting is a challenging sport with important requirements. First of all, planning your trip carefully ensures[1] your safety at all times. Therefore, the river-rafting company you choose should have a good safety record. You can select a river-rafting trip from level I (no experience) to level VI (the most

5   experience). At level I, the river moves slowly and does not have many dangerous rocks and boulders,[2] so you can actually enjoy the scenery. At each level up the scale, there is an increasing number of powerful waves and dangerous rocks. When the river is high from melting snow, the current[3] is fast, and the ride is rough. Therefore, it is only for the most experienced river

10   runner. In addition, river rafting requires special equipment. You ride an inflatable[4] rubber boat with an expertly trained guide and a group of six to eight people. Everyone must wear a life jacket and a helmet and be able to use a paddle[5] at the more difficult levels. Finally, you must be alert at all times. You must stay safely in the raft as it makes its way down the raging[6] river. The

15   guide will shout instructions, and the passengers must obey instantly and work as a team to avoid disaster. The chances of falling overboard are great. When someone does, the passengers will try to grab and pull him or her aboard. Because river conditions can be dangerous at the higher levels of difficulty, the wild, exciting adventure is only for the courageous and experienced. In short, if

20   you are fearless and in good physical condition and can react quickly, river rafting is the ideal outdoor sport for you.

QUESTIONS ON THE MODEL

1. Which sentence explains what the "River Rafting" paragraph is about?

2. What are the three main requirements for river rafting? What transition signals does the writer use to introduce each one?

3. Which supporting sentences explain each requirement?

4. What is the writer's final recommendation to the reader?

---

[1]**ensures:** makes certain, protects; [2]**boulder:** large rock; [3]**current:** continuously moving water; [4]**inflatable:** can be filled with air; [5]**paddle:** short pole with a wide, flat blade used to guide a river raft; [6]**raging:** violent

PART *1* Organization

The Parts of a Paragraph

As you learned in Unit 1, a **paragraph** is a group of related sentences that develops one main idea, which is the topic of the paragraph. Each paragraph is a separate unit. It is marked by indenting the first word from the left-hand margin or by leaving extra space above and below the paragraph. (Refer to Finished Paragraph Format on pages 6–7.)

A paragraph is made up of three kinds of sentences that develop the writer's main idea, opinion, or feeling about a subject. These sentences are (1) the topic sentence, (2) supporting sentences, and (3) the concluding sentence. The writer may add a final comment after the conclusion.

In the paragraph entitled "River Rafting" that you just read, the first sentence is the **topic sentence**. It tells the reader what the paragraph is about: requirements for river rafting. The fifteen **supporting sentences** that follow supply the details about river rafting. The seventeenth, or next to last, sentence is the **concluding sentence**. It makes a final statement about the topic and tells the reader that the paragraph is finished. The very last sentence is the writer's comment about the subject.

Now, let's study each part of the paragraph in detail.

The Topic Sentence

The topic sentence is the most general statement of the paragraph. It is the key sentence because it names the subject and the controlling idea: the writer's main idea, opinion, or feeling about that topic.

The topic sentence can come at the beginning or at the end of a paragraph. You should write your topic sentence as the first sentence of your paragraph for two reasons. First, it will tell the reader what you are going to say. Second, you can look back at the topic sentence often as you write the supporting sentences. It will help you stay on the subject as you write.

The topic sentence is a complete sentence. It has three parts: a subject, a verb, and a controlling idea.

Determining the **subject** of a topic sentence is a process of narrowing down an idea from general to specific. When your instructor suggests a very general topic, such as college, vacations, or nuclear power, for a writing assignment, you must narrow it down to a limited topic that can be discussed in one paragraph. For example, the topic of sports is too general to write about. There are many specific things about sports, such as professional sports, team or individual sports, or water sports, that you can discuss. One writer might narrow down the subject of sports to the more specific subject of river rafting.

sports	water sports	on a river	dangerous	river rafting

PRACTICE:
Narrowing Subjects from General to Specific

Complete each funnel until you arrive at a specific subject. Try to add at least three or four ideas to each group.

1. **science**   **space science**   space exploration   unmanned exploration   Mars probe

2. **family**   **husband/wife**   roles   at home

3. **sports**   **individual sports**

4. **vacation**

The topic sentence of your paragraph must also have a **controlling idea**. The controlling idea is the main point, opinion, or feeling that you have about the subject, and it controls or limits what you will write about it in your paragraph. Putting your ideas in a funnel, as you did in the preceding practice, can help you to arrive at a controlling idea for a topic sentence.

In the example on page 71, the general subject of sports has been narrowed to a specific subject, river rafting. The writer's next step is to decide on a limited area about river rafting that can be discussed in one paragraph.

The following example illustrates how the writer arrives at the controlling idea.

river rafting   **dangerous**   description   making choices   important requirements

Now that the writer has the subject and a controlling idea, she can write a good, clear topic sentence, which will be her guide as she writes the rest of the paragraph.

   Subject   **Controlling Idea**
River rafting is a challenging sport with important requirements.

PRACTICE:
Narrowing Controlling Ideas from General to Specific

In the following practice items, the general idea or subject is given at the widest part of each funnel. Ask yourself questions as you narrow down the ideas: Why . . . ? Who . . . ? What . . . ? Which . . . ? When . . . ? Where . . . ? How . . . ? Add your own ideas to the funnel. Make them more specific as the funnel narrows. Write the most limited idea at the end of the funnel.

1. **college**   **Greenhills College**   registration   frustrating experience

Ask yourself: What is registration like?
               How can I describe it?

2. **classes**   **my best/worst class**

Ask yourself: Which is my worst/best class?
                 Why?
                 How can I describe it?

3. **relationships**

_____

_____

4. **television**

_____

_____

5. **working**

_____

A. Write topic sentences using the controlling ideas at the end of the funnels in the preceding exercise. Remember: a topic sentence is a complete sentence. It must have a subject + verb + controlling idea.

1. _Registration at Greenhills College is a frustrating experience._ _____

2. _____

3. _____

4. _____

5. _____

B. Study the following pairs of sentences and check the one you think would be a good, clear topic sentence for a paragraph. The first one is done for you. Explain your choice.

✔ 1. Snow skiing on the highest mountainsides requires great skill.
2. Snow skiing is fun.

3. Exercise is healthful.
4. Jogging is healthful for several reasons.

5. Camping is a great outdoor activity.
6. Camping requires a variety of special equipment.

7. The legal age for drinking alcoholic drinks should be twenty-one for several reasons.
8. Drinking is dangerous to your health.

9. Small cars are popular.
10. Driving a VW Rabbit saves money.

11. Hong Kong is an exciting city.
12. Hong Kong is a shopper's dream world.

13. The violence on television can affect children's emotional well being.
14. Watching television is a waste of time.

15. Smoking is a bad habit.
16. It is difficult to quit smoking for three reasons.

C. With a partner or a small group, write topic sentences on the following topics. Ask wh-questions to limit the topic and the controlling idea.

> **Example:**   camping
> To set up camp requires a variety of special equipment.

1. sports heroes (who? which sport? why?)

_____

_____

2. spectator sports

_____

_____

3. water sports

_____

_____

4. Olympic sports

_____

_____

5. watching sports on television

_____

_____

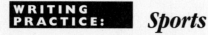

Sports

Choose a topic sentence from part C of the preceding practice and write a paragraph that explains it.

- Brainstorm for six or seven items that will support the topic sentence.

- With a partner, edit and revise your paragraph. Check your own and your partner's paragraph, making sure that your paragraphs each begin with a clear topic sentence that contains a controlling idea.

Supporting Sentences

The next part of the paragraph is the supporting sentences. They develop the topic sentence by giving specific details about the topic. In order to choose details to support the topic sentence, rephrase it as a question, and then answer that question with your supporting sentences.

For example, in the model paragraph you read about river rafting, the topic sentence is

> River rafting is a challenging sport with important requirements.

If you turn that statement into a question, it will say

> What important requirements are necessary for river rafting?

The supporting sentences in the paragraph must answer this question by explaining what the important requirements are. Look back at the model paragraph and complete this list of requirements.

1. Plan your trip carefully. _____

2. _____

3. _____

You can see that the supporting sentences list the important requirements for river rafting.

Another question you can ask about your topic sentence is this one: How can I prove this? Your supporting sentences should give some facts or examples that prove your topic sentence is true.

For example, suppose you wrote this topic sentence:

> Traditional American family relationships have changed greatly in the last thirty years.

You could then ask yourself: How can I prove that this is true? You could prove or support it by giving facts such as these:

1. x out of x marriages end in divorce (in the United States).

2. x out of x children live in homes with only one parent.

3. x percent of couples living together are not legally married.

Still another way to develop your topic sentence is to give examples. Suppose you wrote this topic sentence:

> Tokyo is the most expensive city in the world.

You could then ask yourself: How can I prove it? You could prove or support this topic sentence by giving examples of the cost of different activities in Tokyo such as these:

1. Cost of a dinner at a medium-priced restaurant

2. Rent for an average two-bedroom apartment

3. Cost of a ride on public transportation

4. Cost of a medium-priced hotel room

In short, in order to develop your topic sentence, you must write supporting sentences that prove, or support, your idea. An easy way to do this is to rephrase your topic sentence as a question or to ask yourself: How can I prove this?

PRACTICE:
Identifying Supporting Sentences

A.

Read each paragraph. Then write a question about the topic. Finally, complete the following lists of supporting sentences from the paragraphs.

Mountain climbing is a very dangerous sport with special requirements and strict climbing rules. The first requirement is to complete a course in a certified climbing school, where you learn about mountain conditions and safe climbing. Another requirement is
5 to wear special clothing that is appropriate for the season; a helmet and climbing boots complete your outfit. You must also carry special equipment: iron spikes[1] to hammer into cracks for support and safety and special climbing ropes. In addition to the special requirements, there are also strict climbing rules for mountaineers. You can climb
10 alone or in teams of two or more. When you climb in a team, each person is tied around the waist to the same rope to protect a climber who slips from falling. You climb one foothold and handhold at a time. You must give exact commands and responses to your climbing partners. At all times, you must be aware of falling rocks and
15 boulders, and when you are tired, you need to find a ledge to rest on. Most mountain climbers would agree that mountain climbing has many rewards. The higher you climb, the more beautiful the view is of the valley floor. You can see treetops, rivers, lakes, and distant mountains. Above you, the sky and moving clouds are a spectacular
20 sight. Enjoy the glorious landscape, for that is your reward for having made it to the top of the mountain!

Topic Question: _____

_____

1. There are special requirements for mountain climbing.

 a. *Complete a course in a certified climbing school.* _____

 b. _____

 c. _____

_____

[1]**spike:** long pointed piece of metal like a nail

2. There are also strict rules for climbing in teams.

a. Each person is tied to the same rope around the waist.

b. _____

c. _____

d. _____

e. _____

B.   Skydiving, a wild sport, requires strict training and special
equipment and a plan for jumping out of the plane. This sport is for
people of all ages who are in top physical condition and have strong
nerves. If you qualify, contact a top professional skydiving school for
5   instructions. Before you can sky dive, you must attend six hours of
class lectures about safety and the use of equipment. First, you learn
how to recognize and react to an emergency quickly. Then you do
physical drills that copy the correct body position in the air. After
that, you learn how to steer a parachute. Finally, you learn how to
10   land on the ground without getting injured. The special equipment for
a skydiver includes wearing skydiving clothing: a jumpsuit, a safety
helmet, and ankle-high boots, and a main chute and a second back-up
chute. After you complete the course, you are ready to jump out of the
plane. You board a small plane with several skydivers, the
15   jumpmaster, and the pilot. The plane takes off and climbs to the jump
altitude of about four thousand feet. Once you are outside the plane,
you follow the jumpmaster's instructions: After you let go of the metal
pole on the wing, you fall with a closed parachute for about one and a
half miles at a speed of 120 miles per hour. When you pull the cord,
20   the nylon parachute opens. As you float gently toward the ground,
you enjoy the quiet and beauty of your surroundings and hope you
remember the jumpmaster's final instructions for a happy landing!

(continued on the next page)

Topic Question: _____

_____

1. You have to be in top physical condition and have strong nerves.

2. You must attend six hours of class lectures.

    a. First, _____

    b. _____

    c. _____

    d. _____

3. The special equipment for skydiving includes the following:

    a. _____

    b. _____

    c. _____

    d. _____

    e. _____

4. Outside the plane, you follow the jumpmaster's instructions.

    a. _____

    b. _____

    c. _____

    d. _____

PRACTICE:
*Writing
Supporting
Sentences*

First, read each topic sentence. Then write a question about the topic. Finally, add two more supporting points to each list.

1. Topic sentence: Smoking in restaurants should be prohibited for several reasons.

    Question: Why should smoking in restaurants be prohibited?

    Supporting points

    a. It pollutes the air.

    b. It can affect diners' appetites.

    c. _____

    d. _____

2. Topic sentence: International students have difficulty taking notes in class for several reasons.

Question: _____

Supporting points:

a. The teacher talks too fast.

b. The students have poor listening skills.

c. _____

d. _____

3. Topic sentence: Everyone should consider several criteria[1] before choosing a sport.

Question: _____

Supporting points:

a. They need to decide whether they enjoy exercising alone or with others.

b. They need to consider whether they want to enjoy a sport for recreation or for fitness.

c. _____

d. _____

PRACTICE:
Brainstorming Supporting Sentences

Choose one of the topic sentences below. Brainstorm for about six or seven items to support it. Then work with a partner and review your lists. Decide which supporting items should remain.

Example: Topic sentence:

Snow skiers must take extreme precautions on the slopes.

List some of the precautions:

a. consider the weather conditions
b. consider the slope conditions
c. consider their ability
d. obey warning signs
                    etc.

(continued on the next page)

_____

[1]**criteria:** standards for judging something (singular: **criterion**)

Topic Sentences

1. Snow skiing is an expensive sport.

2. A river runner should follow this procedure.

3. A sky diver must follow these instructions.

4. Camping requires a variety of special equipment.

5. Jogging is beneficial to your health for several reasons.

6. Bicycling provides several advantages.

7. Swimming in the ocean is dangerous for several reasons.

The Concluding Sentence

After you have finished writing the last sentence supporting the main point of a paragraph, you must end the paragraph with a concluding sentence. This sentence tells the reader that the paragraph is finished, and it completes the development of the subject of the paragraph.

The concluding sentence is like the topic sentence because both are general statements. However, the topic sentence is usually the first sentence, a general statement that introduces the topic to be discussed in the paragraph. The concluding sentence is also a general statement, but it is the last sentence and ends the paragraph.

The concluding sentence reminds the reader of the topic sentence. In fact, the concluding sentence can be written like the topic sentence but in different words.

When you write a concluding sentence, you can use one of the following methods.

*   State the topic sentence in different words. **Do not** just copy the topic sentence.
*   Summarize[1] some (or all) of the main points in the paragraph.

You may begin the concluding sentence with a phrase that tells the reader that the paragraph is completed:

All in all, . . .	In other words, . . .
In any event, . . .	In short, . . .
In brief, . . .	Therefore, . . .
Indeed[2], . . .	

Here are examples of topic sentences:

River rafting is a challenging sport with important requirements.

Mountain climbing is a very hazardous sport with special requirements and strict climbing rules.

---

[1]**summarize:** to mention only the most important points; [2]**indeed:** without any question, in reality

Here are the concluding sentences for each of the above topic sentences:

(In short,) if you are fearless and in good physical condition and can react quickly, river rafting is the ideal outdoor sport for you.

Enjoy the glorious landscape, for that is your reward for having made it to the top of the mountain!

The Concluding Comment

After the concluding sentence of a paragraph, you may add a **concluding comment.** This sentence is the writer's final comment or thought about the subject of the paragraph. The purpose of the final comment is to give the reader something to think about and to remember about the paragraph. In the following example, the second sentence is the writer's final comment about river rafting.

Because river conditions can be dangerous at the higher levels of difficulty, the wild, exciting adventure is only for the courageous and experienced. In short, if you are fearless and in good physical condition and can react quickly, then river rafting is the ideal outdoor sport for you.

PRACTICE:
Writing Concluding Sentences

Write a concluding sentence for each of the following topic sentences. You may begin the concluding sentence with a conclusion phrase followed by a comma (see page 80).

1. Writing a paragraph in English is easy if you follow these steps.

   _____

   _____

2. The cafeteria is an inexpensive place to eat.

   _____

   _____

3. My first day of school was a frightening experience.

   _____

   _____

4. Everyone in a car should fasten his or her safety belt.

   _____

   _____

5. Watching television situation comedy is a good way to learn English conversation.

   _____

   _____

PRACTICE:
Concluding Comments

The following scrambled groups of sentences include a topic sentence, a concluding sentence, and a concluding comment. Study each group carefully, and underline the concluding comment sentence in each.

1. You can lose weight if you follow these steps. It will take both time and effort, but the results will make you happy. Losing weight is not difficult.

2. Everyone should be aware of the dangers of heavy smoking. Smoking is the cause of several serious diseases. Smoking can harm your lungs and heart.

3. A working couple should divide home responsibilities. By sharing the work, they will have more time for leisure activities. A husband should be willing to help his wife with the children, housework, and shopping.

4. It is important for consumers to be aware of the dangers of such false advertising. These advertisements carry the message that young people can smoke and still be good looking, healthy, and athletic. Cigarette advertisements try to attract young people in several ways.

5. Take the boredom out of exercising and do it to music. Exercising to music can increase your enthusiasm. Listening to fast lively music while running or exercise dancing will make working out easier and fun.

PART 2 Prewriting *(continued)*

Outlining a Paragraph

An outline is a helpful guide for you to use as you write a paragraph. In an outline, you list your ideas in the order in which you will write about them. Then when you write the rough draft, refer to your outline. Doing so will help you to stay on the topic and to write a well-organized paragraph.

This is what a simple outline looks like:

Simple Outline

Topic sentence
A. Main supporting sentence
B. Main supporting sentence
C. Main supporting sentence
   etc.
Concluding sentence

Turn back to the practice on pages 79–80 on brainstorming supporting sentences. If you made a simple outline for the example in that practice, it would look like the following model.

Snow Skiing

Snow skiers must take extreme precautions on the slopes.
- A. They must consider the weather conditions.
- B. They must consider the slope conditions.
- C. They must consider their own ability.
- D. They must obey the warning signs.

Snow skiing is a safe and enjoyable winter sport if skiers take a few precautions.

A more detailed outline might look like this:

**Detailed
Outline**

Topic sentence
- A. Main supporting sentence
  1. Supporting detail
  2. Supporting detail
  3. Supporting detail
- B. Main supporting sentence
  1. Supporting detail
  2. Supporting detail
  3. Supporting detail
- C. Main supporting sentence
  1. Supporting detail
  2. Supporting detail
  3. Supporting detail
     etc.

Concluding sentence

In this detailed outline, main supporting sentences A, B, and C are the main points of the paragraph. Each of them supports the topic sentence. Supporting details 1, 2, and 3 are the supporting details for each main supporting sentence. Of course, outlines are usually not as regular as this model. Every outline will probably have a different number of main supporting sentences and a different number of supporting details.

This is how a detailed outline for our example about snow skiing might look:

Snow Skiing

Snow skiers must take extreme precautions on the slopes.
- A. They must consider the weather conditions.
  1. Temperature
  2. Wind
  3. Storm or clear weather

(continued on the next page)

B. They must consider the slope conditions.
   1. Icy surfaces
   2. Rocks and tree stumps
   3. Visibility
   4. Crowds
C. They must consider their own ability.
   1. Beginner
   2. Intermediate
   3. Expert
D. They must obey the warning signs.
   1. Out-of-bounds markers
   2. Closed trails and runs
   3. Avalanche danger
   4. "Slow" and "merging" trails
   5. Hazards

Snow skiing is a safe and enjoyable winter sport if skiers take a few precautions.

Using an Outline

After you have prepared an outline, the next step, writing a rough draft, is easy. Because you have already organized your ideas, you can concentrate on writing smooth and grammatically correct sentences. Start with the topic sentence, and follow the points in your outline. Use the outline as a guide. If you want to change something, do so. An outline is only a guide to help you. You should not feel that you cannot add, delete, or change during this step in the writing process.

Here is the final paragraph about snow skiing after it was edited. The topic sentence and concluding sentences are in **bold** type, and the main supporting sentences are underlined. Notice the changes that have been made. The paragraph generally follows the order of the ideas in the outline, but some sentences have been changed. Even the topic sentence is a little different.

MODEL:
Edited Paragraph

Snow Skiing

Snow skiers should take a few precautions on the slopes for their own safety and the safety of other skiers. Before going out, they should check weather conditions. If it is stormy, they may not want to go at all. Extreme cold can be dangerous, especially for beginning skiers, and wind makes skiing unpleasant. Skiers should also know the conditions of the ski slopes. In the early morning, the slopes may be icy. Hitting a patch of ice at high speed

5

can cause hard falls and injuries. If the snow is not very deep, skiers should
watch for rocks and tree stumps. If visibility is poor because of blowing snow
or fog, skiers should slow down. In addition, skiers should ski cautiously if the

10   slopes are very crowded, especially in areas where there are many beginning
skiers. <u>Of course, skiers should consider their own ability and not ski on runs
that are too steep.</u> Beginners and intermediates should not ski down runs
marked "expert" or "advanced." <u>Finally, skiers must obey all warning signs.</u>
Some of these signs warn them about closed trails, avalanche danger, and

15   hazards such as rocks. Skiers should not ski beyond the out-of-bounds signs
because if they fall and are injured, no one will find them. Also, they should
always obey the "slow" signs in congested areas. **If skiers take a few
precautions, snow skiing can be a safe winter sport that can be
enjoyed by people of all ages.** Are you ready? Let's hit the slopes!

PART 3 The Writing Process

Now let's complete the writing process you began at the beginning of the unit.
Write a paragraph about a special sport or activity that you are presently
enjoying, have enjoyed in the past, or plan to do in the future.

STEP 1:
Prewrite to Get Ideas

At the beginning of the unit, you made notes from the list of questions on
page 69. You also made notes as your classmates asked questions and made
comments about your sport or activity.

STEP 2:
Organize the Ideas

First, make a list of the ideas in the order that you will write about them. Then
write a simple or a detailed outline.

STEP 3:
Write the Rough Draft

Write ROUGH DRAFT at the top of your paper.

- Begin your paragraph with a topic sentence that names the topic and controlling idea.

  My drama classes have given me confidence.

  Jogging is my favorite sport for several reasons.

  Stamp collecting is an educational hobby.

- Write a rough draft. Use your outline as a guide.

- End your paragraph with a sentence that tells why this sport or activity is special. Add your final thoughts or final comment.

STEP 4:
Editing the Rough Draft

Edit the rough draft. Follow the editing procedure you used in previous units.

EDITING CHECKLIST

Writer's Questions	Peer Editor's Answers and Comments
FORMAT	
1. Is the format correct?	Check the title, indenting, margins, and double spacing.
ORGANIZATION	
2. Does the paragraph begin with a topic sentence?	Copy the topic sentence:
3. Does the topic sentence have a clear controlling idea?	Underline the topic and circle the controlling idea.
4. Do the supporting sentences "prove" the main idea stated in the topic sentence?	How many supporting sentences are there? Do they prove the main idea? yes no somewhat
5. Does the paragraph end with a concluding sentence?	Copy the concluding sentence:
6. Is there a final comment?	yes no Does it fit the paragraph? yes no

GRAMMAR AND MECHANICS	
7. Is there a period at the end of each sentence?	Check each sentence. Does each one end with a period? yes no Add any missing periods.
8. Are capital letters used where necessary?	Write down any words that should be capitalized and are not:
9. Are commas used correctly?	Circle any comma errors. Add missing commas.
10. Are verb tenses correct?	Underline any verbs that you think are not correct and discuss the correction with the writer.
SENTENCE STRUCTURE	
11. Does each sentence have a subject and a verb and express a complete thought?	Check each sentence. Underline any sentences that you have doubts about.
12. Does each verb agree with its subject?	Write down any subjects and verbs that do not agree:
13. Are both simple and compound sentences used?	Which sentence type does this writer use the most often? Circle one: simple compound other

STEP 5:
Write the Second Draft

Write SECOND DRAFT at the top of your paper. Write the second draft of your paragraph to hand in to your instructor.

STEP 6:
Write the Final Draft

After your instructor returns your paragraph, write a neat final copy to hand in for final evaluation. Write FINAL DRAFT at the top of your paper.

ADDITIONAL WRITING

1. Write a paragraph about a bad habit of one of your friends, a family member, a pet, or yourself.

2. Write a paragraph in which you tell about a pleasant, humorous, or frightening dream.

Unit 5 More About Paragraph Organization

PREWRITING
- *Brainstorming*

SENTENCE STRUCTURE
- *Independent Clauses*
- *Dependent Clauses/Complex Sentences*
- *Complex Sentences with Adverb Clauses*

ORGANIZATION
- *Unity*
- *Coherence*
  Using Transition Signals
  Using Consistent Pronouns

THE WRITING PROCESS

*I*n Unit 4, you studied the structure of the paragraph in detail and practiced writing expository paragraphs. You are now ready to study more about paragraph organization and the importance of having both unity and coherence in a well-written paragraph.

Prewriting: Brainstorming

ACTIVITY

A. Choose either topic 1 or 2.

1. Name an animal or object that is the national emblem[1] of your country. For example, the bald eagle is the national emblem of the United States. It supposedly possesses the qualities of courage, power, and majesty.[2] The Korean flag features the yin and yang circle, which symbolizes creation and development. The flag as a whole represents the ideal of the Korean people to develop forever together with the universe.

2. Name a cultural symbol such as an animal, building, statue, or other object that has national significance in your country. For example, in Japanese culture, the crane[3] is the "king of birds" and is a popular symbol of long life. The carp is the "king of fish" and is the symbol of strength and perseverance.[4]

B. Brainstorm and list as many facts as you can about your country's national emblem or cultural symbol. The following questions are only to help you get ideas for your brainstorming list. Do not write answers.

1. What is the national emblem or cultural symbol?

2. What are its physical characteristics? (The eagle is large and has a heavy hooked beak; stout legs and feet; long, sharp, curved claws; and long, broad wings.)

3. Where is the emblem used? (The bald eagle is on the official government seal, on the ceiling of the Oval Office in the White House, on the top of flagpoles, on the quarter and the one-dollar bill, etc.)

4. What meaning does the animal have? Longevity? Happiness? Prosperity?

5. Do you agree with the choice of this animal as the symbol of your nation or culture? Why or why not?

C. After you complete your brainstorming list, read through it, and draw a line through the items that you will not use.

D. Then work with a partner or small group. Discuss your choice, using your list only as a guide. Your classmate(s) should ask you questions and share information. Take notes about anything new.

E. Save your list and notes. You will use them later to write a paragraph.

---

[1]**emblem:** object that is the sign of something, a symbol; [2]**majesty:** greatness; [3]**crane:** large wading bird with a long neck and legs; [4]**perseverance:** patience, determination

MODEL PARAGRAPH:

Unity and Coherence

As you read the model paragraph, notice the transition words and phrases.

Animals in Captivity[1]

Animals living in modern zoos enjoy several advantages over animals in the wild; however, they must also suffer some disadvantages. One advantage of living in captivity is that the animals are separated from their natural predators[2]; they are protected and can, therefore, live without risk of being attacked. Another

5   advantage is that they are regularly fed a special, well-balanced diet; thus, they do not have to hunt for food or suffer times when food is hard to find. Furthermore, veterinarians[3] give them regular checkups, and whenever the animals are sick, they give them prompt medical attention. Because all of their needs are taken care of, most zoo animals are healthy and contented. On the

10   other hand, zoo animals face several distinct disadvantages. The most important disadvantage is that since they do not have to hunt for food or face their enemies, some animals become bored, discontented, and even nervous. Another disadvantage is that zoo visitors can endanger their lives. Some animals can pick up airborne diseases from humans unless they are protected by glass walls.

15   Furthermore, visitors often throw human food or garbage at the animals. If they eat it, they can become seriously ill and even die. In brief, even though animals in modern zoos live in safe, artificial[4] habitats,[5] life in captivity brings with it a whole new set of dangers. However, zoo professionals and workers always work hard to keep these beautiful animals healthy and contented, and the public

20   should also cooperate fully in that effort.

QUESTIONS ON THE MODEL

1. What is the topic sentence? Underline it.

2. How many advantages does the writer list? Name them.

3. What transition words and phrases introduce the advantages?

4. Underline the sentence that introduces the disadvantages.

5. How many disadvantages does the writer list? Name them.

6. What transition words and phrases introduce the disadvantages?

---

[1]**captivity:** lack of freedom; [2]**predator:** wild animal that kills to live; [3]**veterinarian:** animal doctor; [4]**artificial:** made by people; [5]**habitat:** natural home of a plant or animal

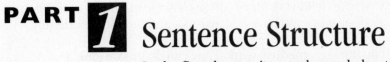

PART **1** Sentence Structure

In the first three units, you learned about simple and compound sentences. In this unit, we will review what you already know and add a little information about compound sentences. Then we will introduce you to a third kind of English sentence, complex sentences.

Independent Clauses

> A **clause** is a group of words containing a subject and a verb. Some clauses can stand alone as a sentence. This kind of clause is an **independent clause.**

A simple sentence is one independent clause.

Tom loves Erica.

1. A compound sentence is two independent clauses joined together by a comma and one of the seven coordinating conjunctions: *and, but, so, or, nor, for, yet.*

Tom loves Erica, **and** she loves him.
Jack loves Jean, **but** she loves Ronald.
Jack should forget Jean, **or** he will die a lonely man.
Jean doesn't love Jack, **so** she won't marry him.

2. Another way to make a compound sentence is to join the two independent clauses with a semicolon. Notice that the first word after a semicolon is not capitalized.

Tom loves Erica; **s**he loves him.
Jack loves Jean; **s**he loves Ronald.
Jean doesn't love Jack; **s**he won't marry him.

NOTE: *Or* cannot be replaced by a semicolon.

3. A third way to make a compound sentence is to join the two independent clauses with a semicolon + sentence connector + comma. A sentence connector is a word such as *however* or *therefore.*

Here is a list of frequently used sentence connectors and their approximate meanings.

Sentence Connector	Meaning
moreover	and
furthermore	and
however	but
otherwise	or, in the sense of "if not"
therefore	so, in the sense of "as a result"

Tom loves Erica; moreover, she loves him.
Tom loves Erica; furthermore, she loves him.
Jack loves Jean; however, she loves Ronald.

Jean doesn't love Jack; therefore, she won't marry him.
Jack should forget Jean; otherwise, he will die a lonely man.

PRACTICE:
Compound Sentences

Combine each of the following pairs of sentences to make a compound sentence. Use all three ways you have just learned, and punctuate carefully.

1. Robots can do boring, repetitive work. They can do unsafe jobs.

   a. _____

   b. _____

   c. _____

2. Robots can make minor decisions. They cannot really think.

   a. _____

   b. _____

   c. _____

3. Robots don't get tired, sick, or hungry. They can work twenty-four hours a day.

   a. _____

   b. _____

   c. _____

4. Human factory workers must learn new skills. They will be out of work because of robots.

   a. _____

   b. (not possible)

   c. _____

Dependent Clauses/ Complex Sentences

A **dependent clause** is a clause (a group of words with a subject and a verb) that does not express a complete thought and cannot stand alone.

There are different kinds of dependent clauses:

1. dependent adjective clauses

which can work twenty four hours a day.
who cannot work around the clock.

2. dependent adverb clauses

before the company installed robots
because production meets buyers' demands

3. dependent noun clauses

that robots are here to stay
whether they assemble watches or lift automobile parts

A dependent clause *must* be connected to an independent clause in order to make a complete sentence, which is called a **complex sentence.**

Independent Clause	Dependent Clause
The company uses robots,	which can work twenty four hours a day.
Robots will replace employees,	who cannot work around the clock.
Production was average	before the company installed robots.
Annual sales are now over one million	because production meets buyer's demands.

The word that begins a dependent clause is called a **subordinating conjunction.** In the examples you just read, the subordinating conjunctions are *which, who, before,* and *because.* The first two signal a dependent adjective clause, and the last two signal a dependent adverb clause. We will study adverb clauses in this chapter and adjective clauses in a later chapter.

PRACTICE:
Dependent and Independent Clauses

Write *independent* or *dependent* in front of each of the following clauses.

_____ **1.** When we arrived at the airport two hours later.

_____ **2.** We arrived at the airport two hours later.

_____ **3.** Because the teacher gave such hard exams.

_____ **4.** After they got married.

_____ **5.** Afterward, they got married.

_____ **6.** Which is not an easy thing to do.

_____ **7.** Which student got the highest grade?

_____ **8.** Who will go to the store?

_____ **9.** While I was a student in high school.

_____ **10.** Where he parked his car.

Complex Sentences with Adverb Clauses

> Dependent **adverb clauses** tell *why, when,* or *where* or introduce an opposite idea.

They begin with one of these subordinating conjunctions:

1. To tell why: *because, since, as*

> **because** all of their needs are taken care of
> **since** all of their needs are taken care of
> **as** all of their needs are taken care of

2. To tell when and where: w*hen, whenever, since, while, as soon as, after, before, wherever*

> **when** they are separated from their natural predators
> **whenever** the animals are sick
> **since** modern zoos have been in operation
> **while** zoo animals are living in a protected environment
> **as soon as** they become sick
> **after** animals pick up airborne diseases of humans
> **before** they become bored
> **wherever** they wander within their habitats

3. To introduce an opposite idea: *although, though, even though*

> **although** animals in modern zoos live in safe, artificial habitats
> **though** animals in modern zoos live in safe, artificial habitats
> **even though** animals in modern zoos live in safe, artificial habitats

A complex sentence with an adverb clause consists of an independent clause + a dependent adverb clause. Most dependent adverb clauses can come at the beginning or end of a sentence.

> **Pronoun Reference**
> When the subject or object of the independent and dependent clauses refer to the same noun or pronoun, put the pronoun reference in the last clause.

Comma Rule

If a dependent adverbial clause comes at the beginning of the sentence, it is followed by a comma and the independent clause

---

Pattern 1: independent clause + dependent adverb clause

> Veterinarians give the animals prompt medical attention whenever they are sick.
>
> Some animals become bored since they do not have to hunt for food.

Pattern 2: dependent adverb clause + independent clause

> Whenever the animals are sick, veterinarians give them prompt medical attention.
>
> Since some animals do not have to hunt for food, they become bored.

PRACTICE:

Complex Sentences with Adverb Clauses

In the following sentences, underline independent clauses with a solid line and dependent clauses with a broken line. Then draw a circle around subordinating conjunctions.

1. (Although) you may not believe it, this is a true story.

2. On August 23, 1994, Tyke, an African elephant, went crazy before she was to perform at the Circus International in Honolulu.

3. Tyke became upset when a caretaker walked behind her.

4. After she picked him up, she threw him into the show area.

5. Because the show was just about to begin, the audience thought the attack was a part of the performance.

6. When Tyke's trainer tried to rescue the caretaker, she crushed the trainer to death.

7. Tyke then wandered the streets for about thirty minutes while police chased her.

8. Before she could attack anyone else, the police cornered and shot her several times.

9. As soon as the bullets hit her, she fell to the ground.

10. Because Tyke was suffering from the gunshot wounds, Honolulu zoo workers injected her with a deadly drug at the scene.

11. Animal rights supporters planned to sue the city of Honolulu and the owners of the elephant since Tyke had previously been violent.

12. In another incident on April 21, 1993, Tyke had reacted violently when someone walked behind her at a circus in Altoona, Pennsylvania.

13. In that incident, she damaged a wall after she ran through an entryway to the circus arena.

PRACTICE:
Writing Complex Sentences

A. Combine a dependent clause from column A with an independent clause from column B and write a complex sentence below. Some dependent clauses can come either at the beginning or end of a sentence. Place any pronoun in the last clause. Use correct punctuation. Write your answers on a separate sheet of paper, and compare them with a partner's.

Examples

before he could swim away   the shark bit John.

Before John could swim away, the shark bit him.

The shark bit John before he could swim away.

A	**B**
1. although many people believe animals don't feel human emotions	a. they clasp hands and call out greetings
2. because they are social animals	b. Sheena watches him with love
3. for example, whenever two friendly chimpanzees see each other	c. chimpanzees feel emotions like joy, sadness, and love
4. after her baby chimpanzee had died	d. she serves as an example of animal emotion
5. before six months had passed	e. Sheena became very sad
6. since Banzo was born	f. that is not true
7. wherever Banzo goes	g. Sheena is quite happy and smiles a lot
8. since Sheena changed after Banzo's birth	h. Sheena became pregnant again

B. Write complex sentences using the given subordinating conjunction.

1. (because) _____

_____

2. (although) _____

_____

3. (before) _____

_____

4. (when) _____

_____

WRITING
PRACTICE: *Sentence Combining*

Work with a partner on this exercise.

1. Combine the sentences in each group into one sentence. There is more than one way to combine some of them.

2. Then write the sentences as a connected paragraph, starting with the first sentence.

How Much Can Animals Think and Feel?

1. Scientists are discovering something.
Animals can think.
Animals can communicate their thoughts.
(Substitute the word that *for something.)*

Scientists are discovering that animals can think and communicate

their thoughts.

2. Gorillas are close relatives of humans.
Chimpanzees are close relatives of humans.
Scientists have worked with them to study animal intelligence.

3. A young chimpanzee named Kanzi knows as much grammar as a two-and-a-half-year-old child.
A gorilla named Koko uses sign language to communicate with her trainer.

4. Most people believe something.
Parrots can only imitate.
They don't understand what they are saying.
(Substitute the word that *for something.)*

5. However, a parrot named Alex talks.
He seems to understand what he is saying.

6. He can answer questions about the color of a toy.
He can answer questions about the shape of a toy.
He can answer questions about the size of a toy.
He can tell what it is made of.

7. Furthermore, Alex can also feel.
Alex can communicate his feelings.

8. Alex made several mistakes in answering a question.
He apologized.
He turned away.
He did this one day. *(Put this idea first.)*

One day, when Alex . . .

(continued on the next page)

9. Alex became sick.
   His trainer had to leave him overnight in an animal hospital.
   This happened another time. *(Put this idea first.)*

10. The hospital was a strange place.
    Alex didn't want to stay there alone.

11. The trainer was going out the door.
    Alex cried out, "Come here. I love you. I'm sorry. Wanna go back."

12. Dolphins also show emotion.
    They do this during training.

13. They are correct.
    They cry excitedly.
    They race back to their trainer.

14. They are wrong.
    They look sad.
    They act depressed.

15. These few examples show something.
    Even animals with small brains are smart.
    Even animals with small brains have feelings.
    (Substitute the word that *for something.)*

PART 2 Organization

Unity

It is important for a paragraph to have **unity.** When a paragraph has unity, all of the sentences in it discuss only one idea. In the model paragraph on page 90, the writer discusses both the advantages and disadvantages of animals in captivity. First, the paragraph discusses the advantages, and then it discusses the disadvantages; it has unity. To discuss anything else about the animals would destroy the paragraph's unity.

Remember: All of the sentences in a paragraph must discuss the same idea. If you start to discuss a new idea, start a new paragraph.

PRACTICE:
Unity

Find and cross out any sentences that do not belong in the paragraphs below.

1.   **New Sports**

As people have more time and money to spend on recreation, new sports are developed. Traditional sports such as racing—on foot, horses, and skis, and in boats, cars, and airplanes—are still popular. Twenty-

five years ago, no one had ever heard of windsurfing. Now it is the
5   rage[1] at beach resorts everywhere. Thirty years ago, who would have
thought that intelligent men and women would jump out of airplanes
for fun, as they do in the sport of skydiving? Twenty years ago, not
many people believed that humans would be able to glide through the
air like birds, as they do in the popular sport of hang gliding.

2.   Modern Zoos

   Zoos are scientific centers with living laboratories. Scientists
conduct important research in reproductive programs in an attempt
to preserve some species. Zoologists can observe the animals mating
and giving birth. The natural living conditions of the various species
5   are duplicated. Moreover, scientists can study the habits, diseases,
and behavior patterns of the animals at different stages in their
lives. That knowledge is used to keep them healthy and contented.
The temperature in the enclosed habitats is controlled although the
outside temperatures vary. Obviously, such scientific studies in zoos
10   are very beneficial for all of the animals.

3.   Automated Customer Service

   Today people have fewer human contacts as they go about their
personal business. To buy gas, you can pull up alongside a gas pump,
insert a credit card, and fill the tank without the help of an
attendant. The charge is made automatically to your credit card. You
5   can pay for your purchase inside the station office. If you want to
make a deposit or withdraw some money from the bank, you can
step up to an automated teller machine (ATM) to complete your
business without talking to a teller. In fact, banking service charges
are rising rapidly. Moreover, to park in a public lot, you drive
10   alongside a ticket dispenser machine, from which an automated voice
explains what you should do. The gate then opens and allows the car
in. When you leave, you insert the ticket in a machine, the gate
opens, and you are on your way. What are the disadvantages of
automated customer service?

---

[1]**rage:** widespread popularity

Coherence

In addition to unity, every good paragraph in a composition must have **coherence.** One way to achieve coherence is through the use of transition signals.

Using Transition Signals

Transition signals are words and phrases that connect the idea in one sentence with the idea in another sentence. They are expressions like *first/second, moreover, however,* and *in brief.* They make the movement between sentences in a paragraph smooth, so the reader does not have problems understanding the writer's ideas. As you will see in Unit 6, transition signals are also used in multi-paragraph compositions to make the movement from one paragraph to the next logical and smooth.

Read the following paragraphs. Is A or B easier to understand? Why?

Paragraph A

Americans love their pet dogs. They do many things for them. They treat their pets like human beings. They like to talk to their dogs and treat them like children. My neighbor Mrs. Green talks to her dog, Ruffy, all the time. She takes him for a walk twice a day. She will not
5 leave him when he is sick. Americans send their dogs to training school to be good and to listen to commands. Americans spend a lot of money on their pets. They feed them expensive dog food with flavors that people like such as beef, chicken, liver, and cheese. Their pets have brightly colored balls, rubber bones, and other toys to play with. In the
10 winter, it is not unusual to see dogs with coats on to keep them warm. Some dogs even wear collars with colorful, sparkling stones that look like diamonds or rubies. Some owners bathe their dogs in the bathtub. Others take their pets to a dog beauty shop. Their toenails are clipped. Their fur is brushed and trimmed. They are given a bath with special
15 dog shampoo. This beauty treatment costs about forty dollars. Americans love their pet dogs a lot. They are willing to spend both time and money on them. They believe that "a dog is man's best friend." Dogs are loyal and dependable and are wonderful companions.

Paragraph B

Americans love their pet dogs, so they do many things for them. First of all, they treat their pets like human beings. They like to talk to their dogs and treat them like children. For example, my neighbor Mrs. Green talks to her dog Ruffy all the time. Also, she takes him for a walk twice a
5 day and will not leave him when he is sick. Moreover, Americans send their dogs to training school to learn to be good and to listen to

commands. Second, Americans spend a lot of money on their pets. They feed them expensive dog food with flavors that people like such as beef, chicken, liver, and cheese. Also, their pets have brightly colored balls,
10 rubber bones, and other toys to play with. Some dogs even wear collars with colorful, sparkling stones that look like diamonds or rubies. Some owners bathe their dogs in the bathtub, while others take their pets to a dog beauty shop. First, their toenails are clipped. Then their fur is brushed and trimmed. Finally, they are given a bath with special dog
15 shampoo. This beauty treatment costs about forty dollars. In brief, because Americans love their pet dogs a lot, they are willing to spend both time and money on them. They believe that "a dog is man's best friend" because dogs are loyal and dependable and are wonderful companions.

Paragraph B is easier to read and understand because the writer has used transition signals. Each transition signal shows the relationship of one sentence to another. Let's review the transition signals in Paragraph B.

- *So* tells you the result (or effect) of the first clause or sentence.
- *First of all* tells you that this is the first example that the writer is going to give of the many things Americans do for their dogs. (The first example is often the most important.)

- *Second* tells you that this is the second example that the writer is going to give.
- *For example* tells you that an example of the preceding statement(s) will follow.
- *Also, moreover* tell you that an idea related to the one you just read is coming.
- *First, then, finally* tell you the time order of the dog's beauty treatment.
- *In brief* tells you that this is the end of the essay.

It is important to use transition signals as you write to connect one sentence with another. You should learn to use them correctly. The following is a chart of some of the common transition signals.

TRANSITION SIGNALS

Usage	Sentence Connectors	Conjunctions Coordinating	Subordinating
To list ideas in time order or order of importance	first (second, etc.) first of all then next after that finally		
To add another idea	furthermore also in addition finally moreover besides	and	
To add an opposite idea	on the other hand however	but	although even though
To add a similar idea	similarly likewise also	and	
To give an example	for example for instance		
To give a cause (or reason)		for	because since as
To give an effect (or result)	therefore thus consequently as a result	so	
To add a conclusion	in brief all in all indeed in other words in short in the end		

Let's review how coordinators, sentence connectors, and subordinators are used to combine sentences.

Coordinators (coordinating conjunctions) make compound sentences from two independent clauses:

and
or
Independent clause, *but* + independent clause.
for
so
yet
nor

I like to swim, **but** I don't like to jog.
Swimming is good exercise, **so** I swim everyday.

Some **sentence connectors** can be used with a semicolon and a comma to join two independent clauses into a compound sentence, or they can be used at the beginning of a sentence with a comma only.

furthermore,
in addition,
moreover,
Independent clause; *also,* + independent clause.
therefore,
thus,
consequently,
on the other hand,
however,

or I hate jogging; **therefore,** I never do it.
I hate jogging. **Therefore,** I never do it.

Other sentence connectors can only be used at the beginning of a sentence and are usually followed by a comma.

All in all, + sentence.
In brief,

In brief, everyone should exercise regularly.

First,
First of all,
Second,
Third, + sentence.
Then
Next,
Finally,

First, bend at the waist, touch the floor, and count to five.
Second, raise your body slowly.
Then raise your hands above your head and count to five.
Finally, drop your arms to your sides.
Repeat the above exercise six times.

(NOTE: *Then* is usually not followed by a comma.)

Subordinators (subordinating conjunctions) are the first words in dependent clauses. A dependent clause must be added to an independent clause to make a complex sentence. Remember that the clauses can be in either order. If the dependent clause is first, put a comma after it.

Pattern 1:

although
Independent Clause + *when*   dependent clause.
because

I exercise every day **although** I hate it.
Walking is good for you **because** it exercises the heart.

Pattern 2:

Although
When   dependent clause, + independent clause
Because

Because I have gained ten pounds, the doctor ordered me to get into an exercise program.

PRACTICE:
Transition Signals

A. Read the model paragraph on page 90 and underline all the transition signals. Refer to the chart on page 102 if you need help.

B. In the following paragraph, choose an appropriate transition signal from those listed after each blank and write it in the blank. In some cases there may be more than one appropriate answer. Capitalize and punctuate correctly.

How Storms Are Named

Have you ever wondered how those big ocean storms called hurricanes or typhoons get their names? Who decides to name a hurricane "Ann" or "Barbara" or "Bill"? The way hurricanes and typhoons are named has changed over the years, and it is an interesting story. Originally, weather forecasters described them by their position in degrees of latitude and longitude _____ a

1. in addition, for example, since.

typhoon might be called "21.20 north, 157.52 west"

_____ this method was confusing because storms

2. then, however, moreover

don't stay in the same place _____ people developed

3. thus, therefore, in brief

other ways to identify them. In the Caribbean Sea, hurricanes were

named for the Catholic saint's days _____ a

4. thus, for example, moreover

hurricane that struck an island in the Caribbean on Saint Ann's Day was named "Santa Ana." A weather forecaster in Australia used to name typhoons after politicians whom he disliked

_____ he wanted to make weather forecasts such as
5. because, for example, however

"Typhoon Smith is on a very destructive path" or "Typhoon Jones is very weak and is not moving in any direction."

_____ during World War I, hurricanes and typhoons
6. in addition, later, as a result

were named according to the military alphabet: Able, Baker, Charlie, etc.

_____ during World War II, women's names began
7. later, then, furthermore

to be used _____ for the next thirty-five years,
8. so, therefore, and

weather forecasters talked about "Typhoon Alice" or "Hurricane Betsy."

_____ in the 1970s, the women's liberation
9. however, then, in addition

movement came along and forced weather forecasters to use men's

names, too. _____ after about 1975, a storm could
10. thus, for example, finally

be named "Gertrude" or "George." _____ the way
11. in short, so, as a result

hurricanes and typhoons are named has changed over the years and

will undoubtedly change again.

c. Add the appropriate transition signals from each list to the following paragraphs, and capitalize and punctuate them correctly. Do not use the same transition signal more than once.

1. To list ideas in time order or order of importance

first (of all)	then
after that	next
second, third, etc.	finally

To apply for a scholarship, follow these steps. _____ get an
a.
application form from your college's scholarship office. _____ fill it
b.
out completely and accurately. _____ ask two of your instructors
c.
to write letters of recommendation for you. _____ turn in the
d.
application form and letters to the scholarship office before the deadline.

2. To add an additional idea

and	moreover
furthermore	also
in addition	

Today it is possible to get many services without making human
contact. For instance, an automatic teller machine (ATM) allows you
not only to withdraw cash but also to deposit funds without talking to
a teller. _____ you can buy snacks and beverages from vending
a.
machines that will accept your money and return any change
automatically. _____ by using your plastic telephone calling card,
b.
you can make national and international calls without operator
assistance. _____ you can earn college credits by taking television
c.
courses instead of going to class.

3. To add an opposite idea

but
however
on the other hand

An American breakfast is different from a Japanese breakfast.
Americans start their breakfast with orange or grapefruit juice or

fruit. Moreover, Americans eat ham or bacon and eggs and toast

_____ the Japanese eat broiled fish, rice, and pickled vegetables.
    a.

Coffee is the beverage for Americans _____ green tea is the
                           b.

favorite drink for the Japanese.

4. To add a similar idea

    and   also
    similarly

I am going to buy either a Rocket Minivan or a Super Minivan.

The Rocket _____ the Super have standard dual air bags. The
           a.

Rocket is equipped with four-wheel antilock brakes _____ the
                                     b.

Super has the newest and best braking system. The Rocket seats five

people in the front and middle seats, plus two more in the rear of

the van; the Super does _____ .
                       c.

5. To give an example

    for example
    for instance

Students are motivated to learn English if they are allowed to be

successful. No matter how small their progress is, each step helps to

develop their self-confidence _____ if an international student has

mastered a difficult grammatical point or can use a new word correctly,

it will help to develop his or her self-confidence and self-respect.

6. To give a cause or reason

    for   since
    because   as

There have been fewer alcohol-related traffic deaths each year

_____ authorities have strengthened existing laws. Alcohol as a
    a.

factor in highway deaths has been declining since 1990 _____
                                               b.

the "don't drink and drive" message seems to be getting through.

(continued on the next page)

This message is aimed at alcoholics, repeat offenders aged twenty-one

to thirty-four, and youths twenty-one and under _____ they

                                                       c.

need to be reminded the most.

7. To give an effect or result

> so
> therefore
> consequently

During the 1960s, a period of noisy student demonstrations,

American colleges and universities had an easy grading system

_____ many students were given more A's and B's and fewer

      a.

C's. Some students still receive inflated grades. However, the faculty

at many schools have called for an end to grade inflation. _____

                                                                b.

students will now have to take their classes more seriously.

8. To add a conclusion

> in short   in the end
> in brief   in other words

_____ it is no longer unusual to see men working as nurses,

secretaries, or nursery school and elementary school teachers.

Generally, less sexism[1] exists in these careers as men have proven

themselves to be as capable as women.

Using Consistent[2] Pronouns

Another way to achieve coherence in writing is through the writer's consistent choice of such elements as person (I, he, she, it, they, you, one), voice (active or passive), and register (formal or informal).

The following paragraph is not consistent in person. As you read the paragraph, notice how the subjects of the sentences change from "a student" to "they" to "you."

Incoherent Paragraph

A *student* who knows a few Latin and Greek roots and prefixes has an advantage over a student who doesn't know them. *They* can often guess the meaning of unfamiliar words. If, for example, *you* know that the prefix *circum-* means "around," you can guess the meaning of words such as *circumference, circumvent, circumstance,* and *circumnavigate* when you read them in a sentence.

---

[1]**sexism:** opinion that one sex is not as good as the other; [2]**consistent:** the same, not changing

In the following paragraph, the problem has been corrected. The subject nouns and pronouns are consistent, and the paragraph has coherence.

Coherent Paragraph

Students who know a few Latin and Greek roots and prefixes have an advantage over students who don't know them. They can often guess the meaning of unfamiliar words. If, for example, they know that the prefix circum- means "around," they can guess the meaning of words such as *circumference, circumvent, circumstance,* and *circumnavigate* when they read them is a sentence.

Remember: Be consistent! If you use the pronoun *I* at the beginning of your paragraph, keep it throughout. If you begin with a singular noun such as *a student* or singular pronoun such as *he, she,* or *it,* don't change to plural *the students* or *they.*

PRACTICE:
Using Consistent Pronouns

A. In each of the following paragraphs, circle the noun or pronoun that is the topic of the paragraph and all of the pronouns that refer to it.

Paragraph 1

Sound requires a definite time to travel from one place to another. The speed of sound in air depends on wind conditions, temperature, and humidity. Sound travels faster through warm air than it does through cold air. It travels about four times faster in water than it does in air.

Paragraph 2

An Olympic athlete must be strong not only in body but also in mind. She or he has to train for years to achieve the necessary strength and control over her or his sport to compete in the Olympics. This requires great discipline and self-sacrifice. Similarly, the Olympic athlete has to train her or his mind in order to compete under extreme mental pressure. This, too, requires great discipline. In other words, an Olympic athlete must be in top condition, both mentally and physically.

B. The paragraphs on the next page lack coherence because the subject noun or pronoun changes within the paragraph. Correct the inconsistent words by making the subjects consistent in person and number. If necessary, change the verbs to make them agree with their new subjects.

(NOTE: Paragraph 3 is more difficult to correct because it contains both active and passive sentences. If you do not know the difference between active and passive, do not do paragraph 3.)

Paragraph 1

Physicists are scientists who are involved in the discovery of the basic laws of nature and the application of these laws to improve the world. They are concerned with scientific wonders as large as the universe or as small as an electron. He or she is a problem solver who is curious about the universe and who is interested in what gives it order and meaning.

Paragraph 2

Many students feel that learning to write well is a useless, time-consuming task that has little to do with "real life"—that is, with their future occupations. While this may be true if he or she plans to become an auto mechanic or a waitress, it is certainly not true if you plan to have a white-collar job. No matter what profession you enter—business, engineering, government—you will have to write.

Paragraph 3

However, the process for writing a composition and, for example, a business report is very similar. First, you collect information. Then the information is organized into an outline. Next, the writer writes the report or composition. After that, it is edited and revised. Finally, you are ready to type it and submit it to your boss or teacher.

PRACTICE:
Adding Transition Signals and Pronouns

Add the appropriate transition words or phrases to show the relationship between sentences. Also, add the appropriate pronouns.

University Professors

University professors have many duties. In the classroom, professors must lecture to the students clearly and effectively.

_____They_____ should encourage the students to participate
   1. pronoun

actively in the learning process by guiding _____ to
                                   2. pronoun

think, to participate in open discussions, and to ask questions.

_____ a science professor lectures in the classroom
   3. example

and in the laboratory while he or she conducts experiments.

_____ _____ supervises students as they
      4. addition   5. pronoun

carry out _____ experiments. Another professor may
           6. pronoun

conduct research in _____ field. _____
              7. pronoun   8. example

Professor Smith did a study of freshmen male college students and

depression. _____ presented the scholarly paper[1] at a
           9. pronoun

conference, and _____ _____ was published
          10. time order   11. pronoun

in a professional journal.[2] _____ Professor Ascher is
              12. addition

writing a textbook for a course _____ is teaching
                13. pronoun

_____ the present textbook is inadequate.
  14. reason

_____ the faculty is required to maintain office hours
  15. time order - last

for student advisement. During this time, students can get help on

difficult material or problems. Professors can _____ use
               16. addition

this time for university-related activities. _____
              17. conclusion

professors are always very busy. _____
            18. contrast

_____ usually enjoy the work _____ it
  19. pronoun   20. reason

brings many challenges and personal satisfaction.

PART 3 The Writing Process

On Your Own!

Now let's complete the writing process you began at the beginning of the unit. Write a paragraph about the national emblem or cultural symbol that has significance in your country.

STEP 1:
Prewrite to Get Ideas

At the beginning of the unit, you made notes from a list of questions. You also wrote down notes as your classmate(s) asked questions and made comments about your national emblem or cultural symbol.

---

[1]**scholarly paper:** long, high-level academic essay; [2]**journal:** magazine

STEP 2:
Organize the Ideas

First, make a list of the ideas in the order that you will write about them. Then write a simple or a detailed outline to organize your thoughts.

STEP 3:
Write the Rough Draft

Write ROUGH DRAFT at the top of your paper.

- Begin your paragraph with a topic sentence that names the topic and tells what it is.

  The national emblem of the United States is the bald eagle.

- Follow your outline and write a rough draft.

- Make sure your paragraph has unity and coherence.

- Use transition signals where appropriate.

- Use a combination of simple, compound, and complex sentences.

- End your paragraph with a sentence that tells why this emblem or symbol is important. Add your final thoughts or final comment.

STEP 4:
Edit the Rough Draft

Edit the rough draft. Follow the editing procedure you have used in previous units.

EDITING CHECKLIST

Writer's Questions	Peer Editor's Answers and Comments
FORMAT	
1. Is the format correct?	Check the title, indenting, margins, and double spacing
ORGANIZATION	
2. Does the paragraph begin with a topic sentence?	Copy the topic sentence:
3. Does the topic sentence have a clear controlling idea?	Underline the topic and circle the controlling idea.
4. Do the supporting sentences "prove" the main idea stated in the topic sentence?	How many supporting sentences are there? Do they prove the main idea? yes no somewhat
5. Does the paragraph have unity?	Cross out any sentences that are irrelevant.
6. Does the paragraph contain transition signals?	Write down the transition signals used:
7. Is the use of pronouns consistent?	Check for changes in pronouns.
8. Does the paragraph end with a concluding sentence?	Copy the concluding sentence:
9. Is there a final comment?	yes no Does it fit the paragraph? yes no

GRAMMAR AND MECHANICS	
10. Is there a period at the end of each sentence?	Check each sentence. Does each one end with a period? yes no Add any missing periods.
11. Are capital letters used where necessary	Write down any words that should be capitalized and are not:
12. Are commas used correctly?	Circle any comma errors. Add missing commas.
13. Are verb tenses correct?	Underline any verbs that you think are not correct and discuss the correction with the writer.
SENTENCE STRUCTURE	
14. Does each sentence have a subject and a verb and express a complete thought?	Check each sentence. Underline any sentences that you have doubts about.
15. Does each verb agree with its subject?	Write down any subjects and verbs that do not agree:
16. Is there a variety of sentence types in the paragraph?	Which sentence type does this writer use the most often? Circle one: simple compound complex

STEP 5:
Write the Second Draft

Write SECOND DRAFT at the top of your paper. Write the second draft of your paragraph to hand in to your instructor.

STEP 6:
Write the Final Draft

After your instructor returns your paragraph, write a neat final copy to hand in for final evaluation. Write FINAL DRAFT at the top of your paper.

ADDITIONAL WRITING

1. Write a paragraph about the most frightening experience you have ever had. Describe the events in the order that they happened. Use the appropriate transition words and phrases. Use simple, compound, and complex sentences. Punctuate them correctly.

2. Suppose friends came to visit you in your hometown or at your college. You want them to have an exciting time. Write a paragraph telling how you would entertain them for a few days. Name some sightseeing attractions and restaurants as well as some exciting night spots that you would take them to. Explain your choices. Refer to the entertainment section of your local newspaper for ideas.

3. Write a paragraph about a current or former job that you either liked or disliked. Begin with a sentence such as *My job as a waitress in the Four Seas restaurant was very stressful/ the best job I have ever had.* Give reasons you liked or disliked your job in your supporting sentences.

Unit 6 Essay Organization

PREWRITING
- *Brainstorming*

ORGANIZATION
- *Overview of Essay Organization*
- *The Introductory Paragraph*
- *Body Paragraphs*
- *The Concluding Paragraph*
- *Transitions between Paragraphs*

PREWRITING (continued)
- *Outlining an Essay*

GRAMMAR AND MECHANICS
- *Present Perfect Tense*
- *Present Perfect vs. Simple Past Tense*
- *Quotations*

THE WRITING PROCESS

*U*nits 4 and 5 taught you how to plan, organize, and write paragraphs. In this unit, you will use your knowledge about paragraphs to learn how to write essays. As you will see, the structure of a paragraph is very similar to the structure of an essay. They are so similar, in fact, that you can almost think of an essay as an expanded paragraph.

Prewriting: Brainstorming

ACTIVITY

Everyone agrees that television has had a tremendous influence on society since it was developed in the 1940s. Some influences have been positive, but others have been negative. With your entire class or in small groups of three or four students, brainstorm the influences of television. Brainstorm both positive and negative influences. Think about how television has changed communication, education, and family life. Make two lists.

Positive Influences   **Negative Influences**

_____   _____

_____   _____

_____   _____

_____   _____

(continued on the next page)

_____   _____

_____   _____

_____   _____

_____   _____

Keep your brainstorming lists. You will use them later to write an essay.

MODEL ESSAY:
*Essay
Organization*

Read the model essay and answer the questions that follow it.

The Computer Revolution, Part I

We live in the age of technology. Every day, new technology appears, ranging from mini-CDs[1] that contain entire encyclopedias to giant space telescopes that can send photographs of distant stars back to Earth. Of all the new technological wonders, personal computers have probably had the

5   greatest influence on the daily lives of average people. Through computers, we can now talk to people in any country, research any topic, work, shop, bank, and entertain ourselves. Personal computers have especially revolutionized communication and business practices in the past twenty years.

Perhaps the most important effect of personal computers has been to

10   expand our ability to communicate with the outside world. A lonely invalid[2] in Minnesota can talk with a similarly house-bound[3] person in Mississippi. Schoolchildren in Manhattan can talk via computer to schoolchildren in Moscow. A high school student can obtain statistics for a history paper from a library in London. A single computer user can send an e-mail[4] message to

15   millions of people all over the world with one keystroke.[5] Computer users can get together in an on-line[6] "chat room"[7] to discuss their interests and problems with others who have similar interests and problems. For example, a person whose hobby is collecting antique guns can share information with other gun

---

[1]**mini-CD:** small compact disk; [2]**invalid:** sick person; [3]**house-bound:** having to stay inside the house; [4]**e-mail:** electronic mail; [5]**keystroke:** pressing of a key, or button, on a computer keyboard; [6]**on-line:** by modem (a piece of equipment that connects computers by means of telephone lines); [7]**chat room:** on-line place where computer users "talk" to many people at the same time

20   collectors via computer. A person who is planning a vacation and wants to know the names of the best beaches in Hawaii can ask others who have already been there for suggestions. People even start on-line romances in chat rooms! The possibilities of computerized communication are indeed unlimited.

Besides improving communication, personal computers have made it possible to do business from home. You can take care of personal business. For example,
25   you can buy airline tickets, send flowers to a friend, pay your bills, buy and sell stocks, and even pay your taxes from your home computer at any time of the day or night. This is a great convenience for people who are busy during the day and for physically disabled people who find it hard to leave their homes. Moreover, telecommuting—working at home instead of going to the office—has become a
30   choice for thousands of business people. Suzanne Carreiro, a financial manager for a large company in downtown Manhattan, has telecommuted from her home in New Jersey for the past two years. She goes to her office only once a week. Four days a week, she works at home and communicates with her staff by computer. She says, "I am much more productive when I work at home because there are no
35   interruptions. I also don't have to spend three hours traveling to and from the office every day. I save myself time, and I save my company money by telecommuting."

In brief, the computer age has arrived, and it is changing our lives. Computers have made communicating and doing business faster and more convenient, and they have greatly increased our access to information. Just as
40   the invention of automobiles had an unplanned consequence—the growth of suburbs—so will the invention of personal computers. We will have to wait and see what these unintentional[8] consequences will be.

QUESTIONS ON THE MODEL

1. According to this essay, what two areas have computers changed?

2. Find two sentences, one in the first paragraph and one in the last paragraph, that name both of these areas. Double underline them.

3. Underline the topic sentences of the two middle paragraphs.

---

[8]**unintentional:** unplanned

PART 1 Organization

Overview of Essay Organization

As you learned in Units 4 and 5, a paragraph is a group of sentences about one topic and has three main parts: the topic sentence, the body (supporting sentences), and the concluding sentence. Similarly, an essay is a group of paragraphs about one topic and also has three main parts: the introduction, the body, and the conclusion. The diagram below shows that a paragraph and an essay have the same basic plan; an essay is just longer.

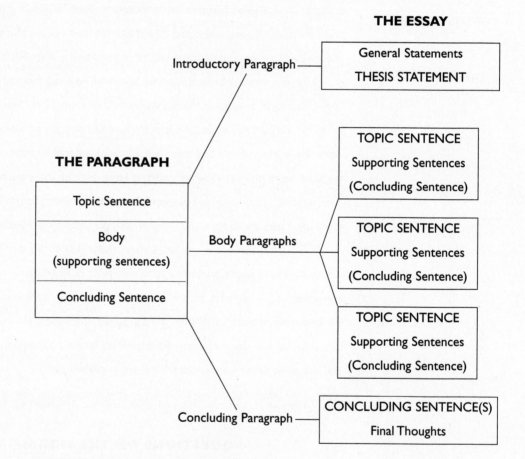

Let's examine each part of the essay.

The Introductory Paragraph

The introduction is the first paragraph of the essay. It introduces the topic of the essay and arouses the reader's interest. There are several ways to write an introductory paragraph. In this book, you will learn to write a "funnel introduction." A funnel introduction has two parts: several general statements and one thesis statement.

General statements give the reader background information about the topic of the essay. They should lead your reader gradually from a very general idea of your topic to a very specific idea. The first general statement in a funnel introduction just introduces the topic. Like the lens of a camera moving in for a close-up picture, each sentence that follows becomes more and more focused on a specific topic. There is no exact rule about the number of general statements you need; however, you should try to write at least three or four, and they should be interesting enough to hold the reader's attention. It is permissible to sprinkle a few interesting details in the general statements in order to attract the reader's interest. However, you should not give any details that belong in the body of the essay.

The **thesis statement** introduces the main idea of the essay.

- It states the specific topic of the essay.
- It may list the subtopics of the main topic.
- It may also mention the method of organization.
- It is the last sentence of the introduction.

Reread the introductory paragraph of the model essay "The Computer Revolution." Notice how the sentences gradually move from the general topic of technology to the specific topic of two areas that have been changed by personal computers. This introductory paragraph resembles a funnel, wide at the top (beginning) and narrow at the bottom (end).

> We live in the age of technology. Every day, new technology appears, ranging from mini-CDs that contain entire encyclopedias of information to giant space telescopes that can send photographs of distant stars back to Earth. Of all the new technological wonders, personal computers have probably had the greatest influence on the daily lives of average people. Through computers, we can now talk to people in any country, research any topic, work, shop, bank, and entertain ourselves. Personal computers have especially revolutionized communication and business practices in the past twenty years.

- The first two sentences introduce the general topic of technology. The mini-CDs and giant telescopes are mentioned to attract the reader's interest.
- The next two sentences narrow the general topic of technology to the specific topic of personal computers. The details keep the reader interested without revealing the essay contents.
- The final sentence is the thesis statement. It names the two subtopics or specific areas changed by personal computers: communication and business.

PRACTICE:
The Introductory Paragraph

In the following introductory paragraphs, the sentences are in incorrect order. Rewrite each paragraph on a separate sheet of paper, beginning with the most general statement first. Then add each sentence in correct order, from the next most general to the least general. Finally, write the thesis statement last.

1. (1) Therefore, workaholics' lifestyles can affect their families, social lives, and health. (2) Because they work so many hours, workaholics may not spend enough time in leisure activities. (3) Nowadays, many men and women work in law, accounting, real estate, and business. (4) These people are serious about becoming successful; they work long hours during the week and even on weekends, so they are called "workaholics."

2. (1) Therefore, anyone who wants to drive must carry a driver's license. (2) It is divided into four steps: studying the traffic laws, taking the written test, learning to drive, and taking the driving test. (3) Getting a driver's license is a complicated process. (4) Driving a car is a necessity in today's busy society, and it is also a special privilege.

3. (1) During this period, children separate themselves from their parents and become independent. (2) Teenagers express their separateness most vividly in their choice of clothes, hairstyles, music, and vocabulary. (3) The teenage years between childhood and adulthood are a period of growth and separation.

Body Paragraphs

The body of the essay is made up of one or more paragraphs. Each of these paragraphs has a topic sentence, supporting sentences, and sometimes a concluding sentence. Each of the **body paragraphs** supports the thesis statement.

Reread the two body paragraphs of the model essay. The topic sentence of each paragraph introduces an area that has been changed by personal computers. Then each topic sentence is followed by several sentences that give specific examples of the changes.

Thesis statement

Personal computers have especially revolutionized communication and business practices in the past twenty years.

Topic sentences

• Perhaps the most important effect of personal computers has been to expand our ability to communicate with the outside world.

• Besides improving communication, personal computers have made it possible to do business from home.

PRACTICE:
Topic Sentence for Body Paragraphs

For the thesis statements on the next page, write topic sentences for supporting body paragraphs. Follow the preceding example. Begin each topic sentence with an order-of-importance or additional idea transition signal (*first, in addition,* etc.).

1. Young people who live at home have several advantages.

   a. _____

   b. _____

   c. _____

2. Owning a car is a necessity for several reasons.

   a. _____

   b. _____

   c. _____

3. Women are superior to men in two ways.

   a. _____

   b. _____

The Concluding Paragraph

The conclusion is the last paragraph of the essay. It does three things:

- It signals the end of the essay.
- It summarizes the main points.
- It leaves the reader with the writer's final thoughts on the subject.

Just as the introductory paragraph has two parts, the general statements and the thesis statement, the concluding paragraph has two parts, the concluding sentences and the final thoughts.

Concluding Sentence(s)

The first part of the concluding paragraph summarizes the main points or repeats the thesis statement in different words. This may require one or more than one sentence. The first sentence of a concluding paragraph sometimes, but not always, begins with a conclusion transition signal such as *In brief* or *In short*. It is not always necessary to use a conclusion signal, and you should avoid the overused phrases *In conclusion* and *In summary*.

Thesis statement

Personal computers have especially revolutionized communication and business practices in the past twenty years.

Concluding sentences

In brief, the computer age has arrived, and it is changing our lives. Computers have made communicating and doing business faster and more convenient, and they have greatly increased our access to information.

Final Thoughts

In the second part of the concluding paragraph, you may write your final comments on the subject of your essay. This is the place to express your opinion, make a judgment, or give a recommendation. However, **do not** add any new ideas in the conclusion because it is the end of your essay. Just comment on what you have already discussed.

Final thoughts

Just as the invention of automobiles had an unplanned consequence—the growth of suburbs, so will the invention of personal computers. We will have to wait and see what these unintentional consequences will be.

PRACTICE:
*Concluding
Sentences*

A. Read the following thesis statements. Circle the letter of the most appropriate concluding sentence. Notice that most of the concluding sentences begin with transition signals although it is not always necessary that they do so.

1. My greatest problem in learning English is oral communication.

   a. Indeed, learning to read and write English is difficult.

   (b.) Indeed, because I do not speak English enough, my listening and speaking skills have not improved.

   c. Indeed, everyone should practice speaking English more.

2. Smoking is unhealthy because it can cause heart and lung disease; moreover, it is expensive.

   a. In brief, buying cigarettes is a bad idea.

   b. In brief, smoking affects your health, and it is also a waste of money.

   c. In brief, smoking is a bad habit.

3. In my opinion, college grades are necessary because they motivate students to do their homework and to attend class regularly.

   a. Therefore, college grades are important.

   b. Therefore, students should be graded for their own good.

   c. Therefore, college grades are important because they cause students to be more serious and to try harder.

4. My major goals are getting a part-time job and mastering the use of the English language.

   a. In short, if I do not reach my goals, I will be unhappy.

   b. In short, finding a job and using English well are important to me.

   c. In short, my major goals are getting a part-time job and mastering the use of the English language.

5. London has excellent bus and subway systems.

   a. It is clear that the public transportation system in London provides reliable service at all times.

   b. It is clear that taking a bus in London is convenient.

   c. It is clear that taking public transportation is a good way to get around in London.

B. Read the following thesis statements. Write a concluding sentence based on the information in each thesis statement.

1. Drunk drivers are the greatest danger on our country's roads.

   Therefore, _people shouldn't drink and drive._

2. There are several disadvantages to owning a big car.

   In brief, _____

3. Smoking in restaurants should be banned because it clouds the air, it smells bad, and it can ruin customers' appetites.

   It is clear that _____

4. Eating in a restaurant is better than eating in a fast-food place because the atmosphere is more pleasant, the food is more delicious, and the food is served to you at your table.

   _____

   _____

   _____

PRACTICE:
Final Thoughts

A. Read the following conclusions. Circle the letter of the most appropriate final thought for each one. Notice the transition signals that introduce the writer's final thoughts.

1. In short, television provides many hours of good, free entertainment that the whole family can enjoy.

   a. However, television can also take over our lives if we do not know when to turn it off. Therefore, we must not watch television at the expense of other activities.

   b. However, violence on television can have a very negative effect on children because they cannot separate make-believe[1] from the real world.

   c. In fact, I like to watch about four hours of television every night.

2. Smokers on the job make it uncomfortable for their co-workers; furthermore, they are less productive on the job than nonsmokers.

   a. Therefore, smoking is bad for everyone's health.

   b. Therefore, smokers should smoke outside the workplace only.

   c. Therefore, if smokers want to get along with their co-workers and improve their work performance, they should stop smoking on the job.

(continued on the next page)

_____

[1]**make-believe:** something imagined or pretended

3. These examples have shown that it is no longer unusual to see men working as nurses, secretaries, and elementary school teachers.

   a. Indeed, there is less sexism in the working world as men have proven themselves to be as capable as women.

   b. So, young boys should be encouraged to go into these careers.

   c. Therefore, women should become airline pilots, bridge construction workers, and symphony conductors.

B. Read the following concluding sentences. Write a final thought based on the information in each concluding sentence. Begin each of your final thoughts with a transition signal like *Indeed* or *Therefore*.

1. Because a working mother has limited time, her husband should help with the children and housework as much as possible.

   _____

2. People who like to get suntanned may get skin cancer.

   _____

3. In short, divorce produces many unhappy, lonely men and women, and it also affects their children.

   _____

Transitions between Paragraphs

Just as it is important to use transition signals to show the connection between ideas **within** a paragraph, it is also important to use transition signals **between** paragraphs to show how one paragraph is related to another. For example, in the model essay, both body paragraphs are about the positive effects of computers. Therefore, the writer uses an "additional idea" transition signal at the beginning of the second body paragraph to show that another positive idea will be discussed. Furthermore, she repeats the first topic (communication) to link the two paragraphs even further.

> <u>Besides improving communication</u>, personal computers have made it possible to do business from home.

She could have used any of the transition signals in the list that follows. The four on the left are sentence connectors, which you practiced in Unit 5. The two on the right are new. The advantage of using the new ones is that you can repeat the topic of the preceding paragraph in the same sentence that you name the topic of the next paragraph. This technique helps link your body paragraphs into a coherent, cohesive essay.

Notice that *Besides* appears in both lists. In the list on the left, *Besides* is a sentence connector and must be followed by a comma and an independent clause. (Turn back to page 91 in Unit 5 if you need to refresh your memory about sentence connectors.) In the list on the right, *Besides* is a preposition. Because it is a preposition, it must be followed by a noun or gerund, which is an -*ing* word used as a noun. Similarly, *In addition* is a sentence connector, and *In addition to* is a preposition.

Study the examples below the chart. In the first pair, the new transition signals are used with gerunds. In the second pair, they are used with nouns.

"ADDITIONAL IDEA" TRANSITION SIGNALS

Sentence Connectors	Prepositions
Furthermore, . . .	Besides . . .
In addition, . . .	In addition to . . .
Moreover, . . .	
Besides, . . .	

Besides suffering from the cold, we also suffered from hunger.

In addition to suffering from the cold, we also suffered from hunger.

Besides the cold, we also suffered from hunger.

In addition to the cold, we also suffered from hunger.

If the next paragraph is about an opposite idea, use one of the following transitions:

"OPPOSITE IDEA" TRANSITION SIGNALS

Sentence Connectors	Subordinators	Prepositions
On the other hand, . . .	Although . . .	Despite . . .
However, . . .	Even though . . .	In spite of . . .

Like the prepositions in the previous list, the two prepositions in this list can be followed by gerunds or by nouns.

Despite being wet and hungry, we continued our hike.

In spite of the rain and our hunger, we continued our hike.

PRACTICE:
Transitions between Paragraphs

Suppose the model essay on pages 116–117 had four body paragraphs instead of two. Add transition signals to the beginning of each extra paragraph to link it to the one before it.

1. The first extra paragraph would follow the paragraph about personal computers and business. Reread the model essay on pages 116–117. Then add an appropriate transition signal to the beginning of this new paragraph, which would begin at line 37 of the model, to show how it relates to the one about business. Does it present an additional positive idea or a negative (opposite) idea?

_____ ,
personal computers have changed the world of education. Elementary schoolchildren are learning to write, practice math, and create computer art. High
school students no longer need to spend hours in the school library xxxx
xxxxxxxxxxxx xxxxxxx. Xxxxxxxxxxxxxxxxxxxxxxxx xxxxxxxxxxxx
xxxxx xxxxxxxxxxx xxx. Xxxxxxxxxxxxxx xxxxxx xxx xxxxxxxx xx. . .

2. Now add an appropriate transition signal to the beginning of the second extra paragraph to show how it relates to the preceding one about education. Does it present an additional positive idea or a negative (opposite) idea?

_____ , not
everyone agrees that computers are good for education. Replacing a teacher
with a machine is not progress, according to some critics. Young children
especially need a real teacher, not a machine, to guide their learning. Xxxxx
xxxxxxxxxxxx xxxxxxx. Xxxxxxxxxxxxxxxxxxxxxxxx xxxxxxxxxxxx
xxxxx xxxxxxxxxxx xxx. Xxxxxxxxxxxxxx xxxxxx xxx xxxxxxxx xx. . .

PART 2 Prewriting *(continued)*

Outlining an Essay

Outlining is an important step in the writing process because it helps you organize your ideas. It is even more important to make an outline when you are planning an essay because you have many more ideas and details to organize.

In Unit 4, you learned how to make simple and detailed outlines for a paragraph. Now let's expand your knowledge and learn how to make an outline for an essay.

As you remember, a simple outline for a paragraph looks like this:

SIMPLE PARAGRAPH OUTLINE

Topic sentence

A. Main supporting sentence
B. Main supporting sentence
C. Main supporting sentence
      etc.
Concluding sentence

An outline for an essay looks like this:

ESSAY OUTLINE

I.   Thesis statement

II. Topic sentence

    A. Main supporting sentence
      1. Supporting detail
      2. Supporting detail
    B. Main supporting sentence
      1. Supporting detail
      2. Supporting detail
      3. Supporting detail
    C. Main supporting sentence
      Supporting detail
(Concluding sentence)

III. Topic sentence

    A. Main supporting sentence
      Supporting detail
    B. Main supporting sentence
      1. Supporting detail
      2. Supporting detail
    C. Main supporting sentence
      Supporting detail
(Concluding sentence)

IV. Topic sentence

    A. Supporting detail
    B. Supporting detail
    C. Supporting detail
    D. Supporting detail
(Concluding sentence)

V.   Concluding sentence(s)

Final thoughts

Notice these points:

1. The topic sentence of each paragraph is given a Roman numeral (I, II, III, IV, V, VI, VII, VIII, IX, X, etc.).

2. Each main supporting sentence is given a capital letter (A, B, C, D, E, etc.). If there are no main supporting sentences but only supporting details, then they are given capital letters as in IV of the preceding essay outline.

(continued on the next page)

3. Each supporting detail is given an Arabic number (1, 2, 3, 4, 5, etc.).

4. Each time the outline moves from a Roman numeral to a capital letter to an Arabic number, the text is indented. Indenting makes it easy to see the movement from big to small, from main ideas to specific details.

5. Letters and numbers are used when there are two or more items in a group. In the essay outline, only one supporting detail is given under II. C and III. A and C; therefore, no numbers are given. However, the single supporting detail is indented in line with the other supporting details that are numbered.

NOTE: An outline is only a guide to help you as you write your essay. It can be changed at any time; that is, you can make additions or deletions to your outline as you are writing.

PRACTICE:
Outlining an Essay

Complete the following outline for the model essay on pages 116–117. Notice that the thesis statement, first topic sentence, and concluding sentences are written out completely. You should write out the second topic sentence completely, but you may use short phrases to list the other points if you wish.

MODEL:
Essay Outline

The Computer Revolution

I. Personal computers have especially revolutionized communication and business practices in the past twenty years.

II. Perhaps the most important effect of personal computers has been to expand our ability to communicate with the outside world.

   A. A lonely invalid . . .
   B. _____
   C. _____
   D. _____
   E. Chat rooms
     (example) 1. _____
     (example) 2. _____
     (example) 3. _____

Concluding Sentence: _____

III. _____
   A. Take care of personal business at home
     1. Buy airline tickets
     2. _____
     3. _____
     4. _____
     5. _____

B. _____

C. _____

(example) *Suzanne Carreiro* _____

IV. In brief, the computer age has arrived, and it is changing our lives. Computers have made communicating and doing business faster and more convenient, and they have greatly increased our access to information.

PRACTICE:
*Outlining
an Essay*

Develop an outline for your own essay.

1. Review your brainstorming ideas from the beginning of the unit. Then prepare a detailed outline for an essay on the positive OR on the negative influences of television. Do not write on both positive and negative influences now. Make sure your outline contains a clear thesis statement, two to four body paragraphs, and the concluding sentence(s) of your concluding paragraph. The body paragraphs should have topic sentences and several supporting points and examples. Use the computer revolution outline in the preceding practice activity as a model.

2. Show your outline to a classmate. Share information, ideas, and examples with each other. Revise your outline if necessary.

3. Plan what transition signals you will use between the body paragraphs. Note them on the outline in pencil.

4. Your instructor may ask you to hand in your outline or to keep it until you write the complete essay at the end of this unit.

PART 3 Grammar and Mechanics

MODEL ESSAY:
*Present Perfect
Tense, Quotations*

As you read the model, notice the verb tenses used. Also, notice how quotations are used to support main points.

The Computer Revolution, Part II

Technology brings problems as well as benefits to humankind. Since Henry Ford began mass-producing automobiles in 1908, they have provided us with a cheap and convenient means of transportation. However, they have also brought us traffic jams and air pollution. A technological development that is

5   changing our lives as much as the automobile is the personal computer. Since

(continued on the next page)

the 1980s, personal computers have become common in homes, schools, and businesses, and just as automobiles have brought unexpected problems, so have personal computers.

To begin with, communication by computer has caused some problems.
10 Although we can easily send a message to hundreds of people in an instant, we can also receive hundreds of messages, both wanted and unwanted, in just a few minutes. A newspaper reporter for the Chicago *Herald-Tribune* recently received more than twelve hundred e-mail messages in one day! It took her several hours to read them. Only a few were important; most of them were "junk mail."[1] She
15 complained, "This isn't the first time this has happened. It's a terrible waste of my time and energy, yet I have to read through all of them because I don't want to miss anything important for a story I'm working on." The lack of censorship in cyberspace[2] is another problem that no one has solved yet. Our expanded ability to communicate means that anyone with a computer can communicate anything
20 to anyone on any subject at any time. Therefore, a computer-literate[3] child can receive pornographic[4] photos and listen to chat-room conversations about sex. These examples show that the computer revolution has created problems as well as benefits in the area of communication.

In addition to problems in communication, computers have also caused
25 problems in business. They have created excellent opportunities for computerized crime. Computer hackers[5] use their skills to obtain secret business information and to steal money. For example, Kevin Mitnick, a computer hacker from California, obtained twenty thousand usable credit card numbers by breaking into the computer files of a credit card company. He also
30 erased the accounting records of another big company before he was caught and arrested. In addition, banks worry that hackers will learn how to transfer money out of customers' accounts into their own. "So far, we have been able to stay one step ahead of the hackers in this particular game," said Charles Buckley, a bank spokesperson, "but security is never one hundred percent in
35 any business."

---

[1]**junk mail:** mail, such as advertisements, that people don't necessarily want to receive; [2]**cyberspace:** worldwide network of computers; [3]**computer-literate:** knowing how to use a computer; [4]**pornographic:** designed to arouse sexual excitement; [5]**computer hacker:** person who tries to get into computer files without authorization

Moreover, the use of computers has depersonalized[6] business. People are no longer customers; they are account numbers. Companies do not seem to care what your name is; they only want to know your number. Face-to-face business transactions are no longer necessary; you can buy almost anything you need by computer, phone, or fax. Also, as telecommuting becomes more common, workers in the same company interact with each other less and less. Someday it may be possible to have a company of people who have never met face-to-face! Is this desirable? Insurance company employee Meredith Bruce doesn't think so. "I feel out of touch with what is really happening in my company, and I miss the social interaction with my co-workers," she says. Social isolation[7] may be an unexpected cost of the computer revolution.

It is clear that personal computers have made our lives easier, but they have done so at a cost. As with every new invention, there have been unforeseen consequences. It is up to us to find the solutions to the problems as well as to enjoy the conveniences of this new tool.

QUESTIONS ON THE MODEL

1. Find and double underline the thesis statement and the concluding sentence.
2. Underline the topic sentences of the body paragraphs.
3. Circle the transition signals.

Present Perfect Tense

The **present perfect tense** links the past with the present.

Use it when the action began in the past and is still continuing in the present. Use it also when the action still affects the present or when it is important in some way to the present in the mind of the speaker.

The computer age has improved our lives in numerous ways. (This action began in the past and is still happening.)

I have never used a computer. (. . . but I might still use one.)

---

[6]**depersonalized:** made less personal; [7]**social isolation:** feeling of being separate from the rest of society

The present perfect is also frequently used for repeated actions in the past.

> There have been several cases of credit card theft via computer. (Repeated action in the past.)

The time words since and yet require the present perfect tense. When since is a subordinator, use the present perfect in the independent clause (not in the dependent clause that starts with since).

> Since Henry Ford began mass-producing automobiles in 1908, they have provided us with a cheap and convenient means of transportation.

When *since* is a preposition, use the present perfect in the same clause.

> Since the 1980s, personal computers have become common in homes, schools, and businesses.

Also, use the present perfect in any clause when *yet* is a time word. Do not confuse the time word *yet* with the coordinating conjunction *yet*.

> **Time Word:**   The lack of censorship in cyberspace is another problem that no one has solved yet.

> **Coordinating Conjunction:**   Computers are useful tools, yet they can cause many problems.

PRACTICE:
Present Perfect Tense

Imagine that you are a well-known television news reporter who interviews famous people all over the world. Think of a famous person about whom you would like to know more, and write five questions in the present perfect tense to ask him or her. Your famous person may be living or dead, and the questions may be serious or humorous.

> (for Queen Elizabeth II of England)
> Have you ever washed dishes?
> How many years have you been a queen?

> (for Yuri Gagarin, first man in space)
> Have you ever been afraid of the dark?

Now, exchange papers with a classmate, and write answers to each other's questions.

Present Perfect vs. Simple Past Tense

> The **simple past tense** is the verb form used for an action that began in the past and was completed in the past. The present perfect is used for an action that began in the past but is still happening or is still influencing the present.

Simple Past	Present Perfect
I lived in Hawaii for three years. (I don't live there now.)	I have lived in Hawaii for three years. (I moved there three years ago, and I am still living there.)
She lived a happy life. (She is dead.)	She has lived a happy life. (She is still living.)
They got married in 1995. (Their wedding was in 1995.)	They have been married since 1995. (They are still married. Remember that *since* requires the present perfect.)
They were married for a year. (They aren't married now.)	They have been married for a year. (They are still married.)

PRACTICE:
Present Perfect vs. Simple Past Tense

In the following sentences, choose either simple past or the present perfect form of the verb in parentheses, and write it in the blank.

1. Van Ng and his family (leave) _____ Vietnam in 1988.

2. They (wait) _____ in a refugee camp in Thailand for six months until they (receive) _____ permission to enter the United States.

3. Now Van and his family are living in Texas. They (live) _____ there since 1995.

4. Before that, they (live) _____ in Minnesota, but it (be) _____ too cold there, so they (move) _____ .

5. Van's father (not find) _____ a job in Texas yet.

6. When they were in Minnesota, he (work) _____ on a dairy farm.

7. Van and his brothers (study) _____ English at a special school for refugees in Minnesota.

8. Since last year, however, they (attend) _____ the local school with American children.

9. Van's older brother is the only one who doesn't go to school because he (graduate) _____ two years ago.

10. A big problem for the Ng family when they first (come) _____ to America (be) _____ the food; they (not like) _____ it.

(continued on the next page)

11. At first, Mrs. Ng (cook) _____ only Vietnamese food for her family.

12. When they (move) _____ to Texas, however, she (become) _____ friends with a Mexican neighbor.

13. Her new friend (teach) _____ her how to prepare spicy Mexican food, and chili con carne (be) _____ a family favorite ever since then.

14. However, they (not learn) _____ to enjoy American hamburgers yet.

15. Although the Ngs (live) _____ in the United States for more than six years, they (not give up) _____ hope of returning to their country.

**WRITING
PRACTICE:**
Present Perfect Tense

Write two or three paragraphs about yourself. In one paragraph, write about your education, both in the past and now. When did you start school? How many schools have you attended? When did you attend each school? What classes have you studied? How long have you been/were you in high school? How long have you attended your present school? How many years ago did you finish elementary school? What did you learn?

- You might write sentences like the following. (Be careful to use simple past and present perfect appropriately.)

  I started school when I was five years old. I have been a student for seventeen years now . . .

- In another paragraph, write about any jobs or work experience you have had in the past.

  Last year, I worked for my father in his business.

- In another paragraph, write about what you have always liked or hated to do. Write three or four sentences to explain why.

  I have always loved to eat. The kitchen has always been my favorite room in the house . . .

  I have always hated to do homework. When our teacher gave us . . .

- With a partner, edit and revise your composition. Check your own and your partner's composition especially for the appropriate use of simple past and present perfect verbs.

Quotations

Direct quotations are often used in academic writing as supporting sentences. In fact, if you use someone else's words in a paper, you **must** use quotation marks. If you do not put quotation marks around the borrowed sentences, you are guilty of plagiarism. If you were writing about the effects of television on children, for example, you could find magazine or newspaper articles on the topic and copy sentences from the articles in your essay, but you must use quotation marks around the copied sentences. Notice how quotations are used to support ideas in the two model essays.

Main point: Telecommuting is a popular new choice for workers.

Quotation: Suzanne Carreiro says, "I am much more productive when I work at home because there are no interruptions. I also don't have to spend three hours traveling to and from the office every day. I save myself time, and I save my company money by telecommuting."

Main point: Telecommuters feel isolated.

Quotation: "I feel out of touch with what is really happening in my company, and I miss the social interaction with my co-workers," she says.

Main point: Banks worry that hackers will learn how to transfer money out of their customers' accounts into their own.

Quotation: "So far, we have been able to stay one step ahead of the hackers in this particular game," said Charles Buckley, a bank spokesperson, "but security is never one hundred percent in any business."

Rules for Using and Punctuating Quotations

RULES	EXAMPLES
1. Use a "reporting phrase" such as *she says, she said, he stated, he added, he continued,* or *they reported.* The reporting phrase may come before, after, or in the middle of the quotation, and the verb may be in any tense that is appropriate. Put commas between the quotation and the reporting phrase. Capitalize the first word in the quotation.	"I love you," **he said.** "I love you," **he continued,** "but I hate your dog." **He asked,** "Will you marry me?"
2. Another useful reporting phrase is *according to* followed by the name of a person, newspaper, magazine, or book.	**According to** graduate student Melanie Wortiska, "Especially useful are news shows such as *20/20* that deal with important issues." **According to** an article in the *Santa Cruz County Sentinel,* "About two-thirds agreed that children their age are influenced by things they see on TV."

(continued on the next page)

RULES	EXAMPLES
3. Give the person's title or occupation if he or she is not well known. In other words, give enough information about the person so that the reader will know that he or she is qualified to speak about the topic. The easiest way to do this is to put the information in an appositive. (Refer to page 154 in Unit 7 for more information on appositives.)	Suzanne Carreiro, **a financial manager** for a large company in downtown Manhattan, complains, "_____ _____." Charles Buckley, **a bank spokesperson**, states, "_____" **Housewife** Jessica Wang said, "_____ _____."
4. Use quotation marks [" "] before and after the **exact** words of the quotation, Notice that both quotation marks go **above** the words, not below them or on the same line. If you omit words from a quotation, put three dots [. . .] in their place. If you add words, put brackets [ ] around the added words.	
5. Put periods inside the quotation marks at the end of the sentence. The period changes to a comma if the quotation comes before the reporting phrase.	She replied, "I don't love you." "In fact, I don't even like you," she continued.
6. Put question marks and exclamation points belonging to the quotation inside the quotation marks no matter where the reporting phrase comes.	He asked, "Why not?" "Because you hate my dog!" she shouted.

PRACTICE:
*Punctuating
Quotations*

Punctuate the following sentences containing quotations. Add quotation marks, commas, and capital letters.

1. Dr. T. Berry Brazelton said the average child today spends more time in front of a TV set than she does studying in school or talking with her parents.

2. as a result he added children often learn more about the world and about values from television than from their families.

3. a majority of child characters on ABC, NBC, CBS, and Fox programs tend to engage in antisocial behavior such as lying or physical aggression reported Scott Dietrich, president of Parents for Responsible Programming.

4. advice columnist Abigail van Buren wrote in a recent column the television set may provide some people with the only human voice they hear for days.

5. it provides news and entertainment for millions of people who cannot leave the comfort, privacy, and safety of their homes she continued.

6. not everyone can attend college in a traditional way says Greenhills College professor Caroline Gibbs so we televise courses that students can view on their TV sets at home.

PART 4 The Writing Process

Now let's complete the writing process you have been working on in this unit. Write an essay about the positive or negative effects of television. Use the outline that you completed in the Practice on page 129 (which was Step 2), and continue the writing process with Step 3.

STEP 3:
Write the Rough Draft

Write ROUGH DRAFT at the top of your paper and write a rough draft from your outline.

*   Add some quotations to support your points. On pages 140–141 are three newspaper articles that you may use as a source of quotations. You may also look for quotations in newspapers and magazines on your own, and you may ask your classmates and teachers for quotable statements.

*   Connect the paragraphs of the body with transition signals.

STEP 4:
Edit the Rough Draft

Edit your rough draft. Follow the editing procedure you used in previous units.

EDITING CHECKLIST

Writer's Questions	Peer Editor's Answers and Comments
FORMAT	
1. Is the format correct?	Check the title, indenting, margins, and double spacing.
ORGANIZATION	
2. Does the essay have an introduction, a body, and a conclusion?	How many paragraphs does the essay have? How many paragraphs are in the body?
Introduction **3.** Do the general statements • give background information?	How many general statements are there? Is this a funnel introduction? yes no
• attract the reader's attention?	Does it stimulate your interest in the topic? yes no
4. Does the thesis statement state a clearly focused main idea for the whole essay?	Copy the thesis statement here:
Body **5.** Does each body paragraph have • a clearly stated topic sentence with a main (controlling) idea?	Write the main idea for each body paragraph:
• good development with sufficient supporting details (facts, examples, and quotations)?	List one supporting detail from each body paragraph:
• unity (one idea per paragraph)?	Underline any sentences that break the unity.
• coherence (logical organization, transition words, and consistent pronouns)?	List the transitions between each body paragraph:
Conclusion **6.** Does the conclusion • restate your thesis or summarize your main points?	What kind of conclusion does the essay have? (Check one.) _____ summary of the main points
• give your final thoughts on the subject of your essay?	_____ restatement of the thesis

GRAMMAR AND MECHANICS	
7. Are quotations used correctly?	Check each quotation for commas, capital letters, and quotation marks
8. Are commas used where necessary?	Circle any comma errors. Add missing commas.
9. Are verb tenses used appropriately?	Check each verb for the appropriate tense. Circle any that you have questions about.

SENTENCE STRUCTURE	
10. Do all sentences contain at least one subject and one verb and express a complete thought?	Underline any sentences that you have questions about.
11. Does the essay contain a variety of sentence types?	What sentence type does this writer use the most often? Circle one: simple compound complex

STEP 5:
Write the Second Draft

Write SECOND DRAFT at the top of your paper. Write the second draft of your essay to hand in to your instructor.

STEP 6:
Write the Final Draft

After your instructor returns your essay, write a neat final copy to hand in for final evaluation. Write FINAL DRAFT at the top of your paper.

ADDITIONAL WRITING

Write about the changes that an invention has already caused or will cause in the future. You might write about the automobile, the telephone, the cellular telephone, plastics, artificial hearts, respirators ("breathing machines"), organ transplant technology, genetic engineering, or any other technological device or process that you know about.

Use these articles for Step 3 on page 137.

DOES TV TEACH VIOLENCE?

A law was passed in the United States in 1996 requiring television sets in the future to have V-chips. These are small devices that allow parents to block out programs containing violence or other content that parents do not want their children to see. This law was passed because research shows that violence on TV has a harmful effect on children.

Scientists studied a remote[1] village in Canada that didn't have television until 1973. They measured the rates of physical aggression among forty-five first- and second-grade boys and girls before television came to the village. Then they measured the rates two years later. After two years of television, the rate increased by 160 percent.

Other researchers studied third-, fourth-, and fifth-grade boys in two other communities in Canada. One got television in 1973, and the other in 1977. The aggressiveness of boys in the first community increased immediately after television came to the community, and in the second, it increased four years after television came.

The nation of South Africa had no television until 1975. Brandon Centerwall, a professor at the University of Washington, studied violence in that country, the United States, and Canada. From 1945 to 1974 the murder rate among white people in the United States increased 93 percent and in Canada 92 percent. In South Africa, it decreased 7 percent. ◆

Dayton Daily News

Kids Criticize TV

Youngsters think television is a bad teacher when it comes to morality and ethics, according to a survey released Monday. The nationwide survey asked youths aged ten to sixteen to describe how television shapes their values.

About two-thirds agreed that children their age are influenced by things they see on TV. Eighty-two percent thought TV entertainment shows should help teach right from wrong.

Older children said television encourages them to experiment with sex too soon and to disrespect their parents. "I think it pressures people my age," said a fourteen-year-old girl.

TV TODAY MAGAZINE

"When they see it on TV, they want to do it, too."

Seventy-six percent said television shows sex before marriage too often. Sixty-two percent said sex on TV and in movies influences kids in their age group to have sexual relations when they are too young.

Two-thirds said that programs with hostile[2] families, such as *The Simpsons* and *Married . . .With Children,* encourage young viewers to disrespect their parents.

Some television officials said teaching values is the job of parents. "Television is entertainment," said Leslie Ray, executive producer of *Fresh Prince of Bel-Air.* "It's not our responsibility to police what children watch. Our job is to entertain." ●

[1] **remote:** far away; [2] **hostile:** unfriendly

Does TV Improve the Quality of Life?

Interviews with Americans

Harry Wang, grocery store manager:

With proper programming, TV can be good. Educational channels are excellent. You can learn about foreign cultures, wild animals, and all sorts of things from the comfort of your living room. Children's educational shows such as *Sesame Street* are good, too. My daughter learned her ABC's from watching Big Bird and his friends.

Jessica Wang, housewife:

No! Television is destroying family life. Now families just sit like robots in front of the boob tube[3] instead of talking or playing games together. Some families even eat dinner in front of the TV screen. There's little communication between parents and their children or even between husband and wife except maybe an argument about whether to watch *Monday Night Football* or *E.R.*

Angela Russell, nurse:

TV is a great source of entertainment and companionship for old people. My eighty-six-year-old mother is in a wheelchair and has nothing to do all day. She loves watching the soap operas in the morning and the game shows in the afternoon. Without them, she would really be bored. I think these programs keep her mind active.

Jacques Camembert, recent immigrant:

Television is helping me and my family learn English more quickly. When we first came to the United States, we could not understand anything. We stayed in our apartment and watched television all day. At first, we watched children's shows, which were easier to understand. Now we can understand a lot more. We are learning the way Americans really talk, not "textbook" English.

George Russell, engineer:

You bet! My kids have learned so much from watching educational programs such as *Wild Animal Kingdom* and the *National Geographic* specials. My son became interested in science from watching *Star Trek,* and my daughter wants to become a veterinarian because of *All Creatures Great and Small.*

---

[3]**boob tube:** television set (slang)

Unit 7 Logical Division of Ideas

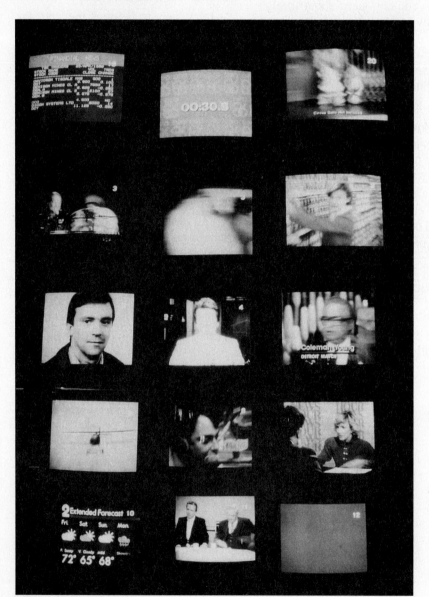

PREWRITING
- *Grouping Ideas Logically*

ORGANIZATION
- *Logical Division of Ideas*
- *Developing a Logical Division Topic*
- *Using Examples for Support*

GRAMMAR AND MECHANICS
- *Restrictive and Nonrestrictive Appositives*
- *Restrictive and Nonrestrictive Adjective Clauses*

SENTENCE STRUCTURE
- *Complex Sentences with Adjective Clauses*

THE WRITING PROCESS

*I*n this unit, you will expand your knowledge of essay writing. You will learn how to organize a large, complex topic by grouping ideas together and discussing each group in a separate paragraph. This method of organization, called logical division of ideas, is useful for many kinds of writing, from business letters and memos to college essays and research papers.

Prewriting: Grouping Ideas Logically

ACTIVITY

Work with a partner or a small group.

A. Divide the following list of words into logical groups or categories according to the chart. Write each word under the appropriate category name.

Shopping in a Supermarket

aspirin	cheese	cookies	tomatoes
bread	lettuce	eggs	steak
apples	potatoes	hamburger	cake
carrots	vitamins	pork chops	toothpaste
oranges	pie	shampoo	doughnuts
milk			

Produce	Dairy Products	Meat	Baked Goods	Personal Care/ Health Products

B. Divide the list of sports on the next page into groups. There is more than one possible way to divide the list. First, decide with your partner or group what your categories will be and label the chart. You may have more or fewer categories than there are columns in the chart. If you need more columns or more space in each column, add them.

(continued on the next page)

Sports

baseball	gymnastics	mountain climbing	table tennis
bobsledding	hiking	scuba diving	tennis
bowling	ice hockey	skiing	volleyball
fishing	ice skating	soccer	waterskiing
golf	jogging	swimming	windsurfing

C. Make a list of English-language television programs that you and your classmate(s) watch.

Television Programs

_____ _____ _____

_____ _____ _____

_____ _____ _____

_____ _____ _____

_____ _____ _____

_____ _____ _____

Divide your list into four or five groups, and give each group a name. Write the name of each group across the top, and then fill in the chart. Here are some possible group names:

news programs	documentaries[1]
children's educational programs	docu-dramas[2]
children's entertainment	crime shows
cartoons	soap operas[3]
adult educational programs	family sitcoms[4]
quiz shows	sports shows

D. Save your chart. You will use it later to write an essay.

---

[1]**documentary:** program that presents factual information; [2]**docu-drama:** program that presents a dramatization of true events; [3]**soap opera:** daily program that presents a continuing dramatic story about the characters' lives; [4]**family sitcoms** (family situation comedies): weekly programs that show families in funny situations

MODEL
ESSAY:

*Logical Division
of Ideas*

As you read the model essay, notice its organization. Try to outline the essay in your mind. Also, notice the transition signals at the beginning of each body paragraph.

Styles of Rock and Roll Music

There is no stopping rock and roll. Since its birth in the fifties, rock and roll has become the most lively force in popular culture. It was born as a child of jazz, blues, and country music. More recently, it has been influenced by movies, television, sex, drugs, art, literature, and electronics. Since its birth, rock
5 and roll has grouped and regrouped into an explosion of styles: folk rock, soul, Motown, hard rock, jazz rock, country rock, heavy metal, punk rock, reggae, new wave, rap, and so on. Each type has its own style, themes,[1] and stars. Three of the more successful styles are rap, heavy metal, and reggae.

One of the newer styles of rock and roll is rap. Rap is a form of dance
10 music in which the singers — rappers — speak in rhythm and rhyme rather than sing. Rap first appeared in the mid-seventies in the discos of New York City's black neighborhoods. Disco DJs[2] teamed up with rappers to play songs for dancers at parties. At first, the role of the rapper was to keep the beat[3] going with hand claps while the DJ changed records. Soon, rappers added lyrics,[4]
15 slogans,[5] rhymes, and call-and-response exchanges with the audience. Early rap songs were mainly about dancing, partying, and the romantic adventures of the rappers, but politics became an important theme in the late eighties and nineties. Although rap is primarily the music of young black males, the first white rappers appeared in 1980, and a woman rapper, Queen Latifah, began her career
20 in 1989. M. C. Hammer's 1990 album, *Please Hammer Don't Hurt 'Em,* has sold fifteen million copies, making it the best-selling rap album of the decade.

Another style of rock and roll music is heavy metal. Quite different from rap, heavy metal is a style of rock and roll that uses highly amplified[6] electric guitars for its sound. It was born in the early sixties when American and British
25 guitarists started putting distortion[7] into their music. The most successful bands have had the fastest and most creative guitarists: Jimi Hendrix, Ted

(continued on the next page)

Source: *The New Rolling Stone Encyclopedia of Rock & Roll (Completely Revised & Updated).* Edited by Patricia Romanowski and Holly George-Warren. New York: Fireside, 1995.; [1]**theme:** topic of a song; [2]**DJ** (disc jockey): person who plays records, tapes, or CDs for dancers; [3]**beat:** rhythm; [4]**lyrics:** words to songs; [5]**slogan:** phrase used repeatedly, such as in advertising; [6]**amplified:** made louder; [7]**distortion:** abnormal, unnatural sound

Nugent, and Eddie Van Halen. Almost as important as the guitarists are the singers, who have great theatrical ability, vocal range, and sex appeal. In the seventies, heavy metal bands turned to outdoor sports arenas, staging

30 elaborate concerts with light shows and amplified sound. Popular heavy metal bands include Led Zeppelin, Mötley Crüe, Poison, Guns 'n Roses, and Metallica.

A third style of rock and roll is reggae, which was born on the Caribbean island of Jamaica in the sixties and spread throughout the world in the seventies. It developed from a kind of Afro-Caribbean music called *mento*,

35 which was sung and played on guitars and drums. Some musicians changed *mento* into a music style called *ska* by adding a hesitation beat.[1] A few years later, other musicians changed *ska*, and reggae was born. Reggae's special sound comes from reversing the roles of the instruments: The guitar plays the rhythm and the bass[2] plays the melody.[3] An important influence on reggae music was

40 the Rastafarian cult.[4] The Rastafarians added unusual sound mixes, extra-slow tempos, strange lyrics, and mystical-political themes. The best-known reggae musician in the United States is the late[5] Bob Marley.

Rock and roll music is constantly changing. New styles are born, grow, change, and produce offshoots,[6] which in turn grow, change, and produce

45 offshoots. Some styles enjoy lasting popularity, but others disappear rather quickly. However, all contribute to the power and excitement of rock and roll music in our time.

QUESTIONS ON THE MODEL

1. How many different rock and roll styles are discussed in the model essay? What are they? In which sentence are three of the styles named?

2. How many body paragraphs are there? What is the topic of each one? Underline the topic sentences.

3. Circle the transition words and phrases that connect the body paragraphs.

4. What information is given in the supporting sentences about each style of rock and roll? Name at least three kinds of information. (Example: how it started.)

---

[1]**hesitation beat:** rhythm in which one beat comes later than expected; [2]**bass:** musical instrument; [3]**melody:** pattern of sounds that make a song; [4]**cult:** religious group; [5]**the late (+ person's name):** no longer living; dead; [6]**offshoot:** branch

PART *1* Organization

Logical Division of Ideas

When you write an essay, you must divide your topic into paragraphs. One method of dividing a topic is to use time order. For example, you could write about the breakup of the Soviet Union by telling the events in the order that they happened, writing about each separate event in a separate paragraph. Another method of dividing this topic might be to write about the various causes of the breakup. To do this, you would group them into social, political, and economic causes and write about each group separately.

Dividing a topic by grouping ideas that have something in common is called **logical division of ideas.** You can organize the information on many topics by this method. For example, you can divide the topic of sports into individual sports and team sports; or summer, winter, and year-round sports; or sports played with a ball and sports played without a ball; and so on.

Developing a Logical Division Topic

After you have divided your topic into groups, the next step is to explain or define each group. For example, suppose you were writing a logical division essay on the topic "Kinds of Lies." You might first divide your topic into "good" lies and "bad" lies. Since there is more than one kind of good lie and more than one kind of bad lie, you could then divide both of these further. Each kind of lie could become the topic of one body paragraph.

Here are three body paragraphs, each explaining a different kind of bad lie. Notice that each one begins with a topic sentence that (1) names the kind of lie and (2) explains what it is. Then one or two examples follow. Each paragraph ends with a concluding sentence that further explains the kind of lie.

Thesis: There are three kinds of bad lies.

Body Paragraph I
The first kind of bad lie is the self-protective lie. Its purpose is to protect the liar from being blamed or punished. Children often tell this kind of lie to avoid getting into trouble: "I didn't throw the rock. I don't know how the window got broken." Telling a police officer that you were going only thirty-five miles per hour when you were really going sixty is another example of this kind of lie. Even though these self-protective lies do not harm anyone else, they damage the liar's credibility.[7]

Body Paragraph 2
A slightly different kind of bad lie is the kind that people tell to gain some advantage for themselves over others. For instance, John exaggerates[8] his salary and responsibilities on a previous job when he applies for a new job. This kind of lie may or may not harm someone else. The company that hires John might find that he is perfect for the job. On the other hand, the company might find that he is unqualified. Then the company would have to hire someone else after spending a lot of time and money to train John. Moreover, the job applicants who were honest but who didn't get hired definitely suffered harm from John's lies.

---

[7]**credibility:** ability to be believed by others; [8]**exaggerates:** says something is bigger, better, or more important than it really is

Body Paragraph 3

The worst kind of bad lie, however, is the kind people intentionally tell in order to hurt or cause trouble for another person. For example, if the boy who broke the window says that another boy threw the rock, he is guilty of telling this kind of lie. Another example of this kind of lie is malicious gossip: "I heard that her new boyfriend just got out of jail," or "I saw his girlfriend at the disco with another guy last night." This kind of lie definitely harms other people; in fact, that is its purpose.

Using Examples for Support

Whenever you make a statement that is not an obvious truth, you need to prove it. One way to prove that a statement is true is to support it with examples:

Suppose you wrote this thesis sentence:

Manhattan is a wonderful place to visit if you are planning a trip to the United States.

If your readers have never been to Manhattan, you will have to convince them that Manhattan is worth visiting. To convince them, you could describe some of Manhattan's tourist attractions. These would be examples.

   I. Manhattan has many tourist attractions. (topic sentence)
     A. Greenwich Village (example)
     B. Statue of Liberty (example)
     C. Central Park (example)
     D. Chinatown (example)
     E. Times Square (example)

In another paragraph, you could write about the variety of fine restaurants in Manhattan.

   II. Furthermore, there is an unlimited selection of fine restaurants in Manhattan. (topic sentence)
     A. French–Les Pyrenees (example)
     B. Italian–La Scala (example)
     C. Chinese–Ruby Foo's (example)
     D. Japanese–Benihana of Tokyo (example)
     E. Thai–Bangkok 54 (example)

You could also write about the excellent shopping, hotels, or cultural events. You would write a separate paragraph for each topic and give specific examples of shops, hotels, and theaters and concert halls.

Examples don't have to be proper nouns, of course. They can also be statements of fact. For instance, you would have to use facts to prove statements such as the following:

   I. The Earth is getting warmer at an alarming rate. (topic sentence)

These two examples are facts that support the topic sentence.

     A. Since 1880, global temperatures have risen about 5 degrees Celsius.
     B. Eight of the twelve years between 1980 and 1992 were the hottest in the 115-year history of global measurement.

PRACTICE:
Examples

Individually or in groups, think of examples to support the following statements (whether you agree with them or not.)

Group A–Use single nouns as examples.

I. Some of the world's strongest leaders have been women.
  A. Indira Gandhi
  B.
  C.
  D. (add more if you can)

II. Certain automobiles are popular because they are economical.
  A.
  B.
  C. (add more if you can)

Group B–Use complete sentences as supporting examples.

I. Young people today are under more stress than their parents were.
  A. They face more competition in school.
  B.
  C. (add more if you can)

II. Drug abuse is not the only problem among today's youth.
  A.
  B.
  C.

Introducing Examples

You can introduce examples in your paragraphs by using one of the following phrases:

For example, _____ (sentence) _____ .

For instance, _____ (sentence) _____ .

For example and *for instance* are interchangeable and can come at the beginning, in the middle, or at the end of a sentence. Notice the commas in these examples:

For example, teenagers today have to study harder in school.
or
Teenagers today, for example, have to study harder in school.
or
Teenagers today have to study harder in school, for instance.

You can also use these structures with examples.

One
Another
An
A second
A third
} example of _____ (noun phrase) is (noun phrase) _____ .

_____ (noun phrase) _____ is an example of

_____ (noun phrase or clause) _____ .

. . . such as _____ (noun phrase) _____ . . .

(continued on the next page)

One example of a nearby tourist attraction is Lake Tahoe, where one can look at beautiful scenery or gamble in busy casinos.

Indira Gandhi, who was prime minister of India for a total of fifteen years, is an example of a woman who led her nation during difficult times.

New York's excellent Chinese restaurants, such as Ruby Foo's, are famous around the world.

PRACTICE:
Developing Logical Division Paragraphs

Work with a partner or a small group.

1. Brainstorm the other kind of lies, "good" lies. How many different kinds of good lies can you think of? Brainstorm at least two different kinds of good lies. Give a name to each kind and develop a brief explanation of it. Then think of examples for each kind.

2. Make simple outlines in the lines that follow. If your group thinks of a third kind of good lie, write another outline on a separate piece of paper.

Good Lies—Type 1

Topic Sentence:

_____

Explanation:

_____

_____

_____

Examples:

a. _____

b. _____

Good Lies—Type 2

Topic Sentence:

_____

Explanation:

_____

_____

_____

Examples:

a. _____

b. _____

Logical Division of Ideas Group Essay

Work with a group of four to six students and write a four- or five-paragraph logical division essay on the topic "Kinds of Good Lies." A different student will write each paragraph, and one student will prepare the outline.

1. Discuss as a group ways to write a funnel introduction (see page 119). After your discussion, assign one person to write the introductory paragraph.

2. Discuss as a group ways to write a concluding paragraph. Assign one person to write the conclusion.

3. Assign a different student to write each body paragraph.

4. Assign one student to write a detailed outline.

5. After you have completed your rough drafts, edit and revise each paragraph in your group. Exchange papers and check each other's work. Check each body paragraph especially for adequate supporting examples. Make any necessary corrections or revisions. Then combine your paragraphs into one essay, and check it for completeness and coherence. Refer to the Editing Checklist on pages 138–139. Finally, check the outline and clip it to the essay before handing it in.

PART 2 Grammar and Mechanics

MODEL ESSAY:

Appositives and Adjective Clauses

As you read the model essay, look for sentences that contain the words *who, which, in which, on which,* and *that.* Underline the clauses that begin with these words.

Kinds of Holidays

Every culture in the world has special days that people observe with traditional foods, customs, and events. The origin of holidays and of the customs associated with them is a fascinating subject. Almost all of them began as pagan[1] festivals, anniversaries of important historical or political events, or religious days.

5   One group of holidays began as pagan festivals in which people celebrated the beginning of spring. The beginning of spring was often the beginning of the new year. Such celebrations still take place in many cultures. A very clear example of a modern holiday with pagan origins is No Rooz, Iranian New Year, which begins on the first day of spring. Iranians celebrate the passing of the old year with bonfires

10   and the entrance of the new year with special foods. They set up a special table on

(continued on the next page)

[1]**pagan:** not religious

which they display seven foods with names beginning with the letter *s* in Farsi, the language of Iran. The seven foods represent life, health, wealth, abundance, love, patience, and purity. Other objects representing a good year—a mirror, candles, eggs, and a goldfish—are put on the table with the seven foods. Another example

15   of a modern holiday with pagan origins is American Halloween, which is on October 31. On Halloween night, children dress up in costumes and go from

house to house to get candy. The children often dress up as witches,[1] ghosts,[2] or

black cats. People also carve[3] frightening faces in pumpkins[4] and put candles inside

them at night. All of these customs started hundreds of years ago in Ireland and

20 England. There, people celebrated the end of the farming season by lighting

bonfires. They also dressed up as ghosts to frighten away bad spirits, which they

believed came back to Earth on that night.

Another group of holidays celebrates important historical or political events.

National independence days, such as July 1 in Canada and July 4 in the United

25 States, are in this category. Mexicans celebrate their victory over the French on

May 5, Cinco de Mayo in Spanish. Furthermore, almost all countries celebrate the

birthdays of their greatest leaders. For example, people in the United States have a

holiday in February to celebrate the birthdays of the two great presidents George

Washington and Abraham Lincoln. Finally, various patriotic holidays belong in this

30 group. In the United States, people who died in wars are honored on Memorial

Day, and people who fought and survived are honored on Veterans' Day.

A final category of holidays includes all of those holidays that have

religious origins. Moslems, for example, celebrate Eid, which comes at the end

of a month of fasting[5] called Ramadan. Buddhists in Japan have a flower festival

35 and parade on April 8 to celebrate Buddha's birthday. The Jewish religion has

many important celebrations such as Rosh Hashanah, Passover, and Hanukkah.

Christians celebrate the birth of Jesus at Christmas and his resurrection[6] at

Easter. Valentine's Day, a popular day for friends and lovers to exchange cards

and gifts, honors a Christian holy man named Saint Valentine.

40 The word *holiday* is a combination of the words *holy* and *day*, but as we have

seen, not all holidays are religious. They may also be pagan or patriotic in origin.

QUESTIONS ON THE MODEL

1. How many different types of holidays does the writer discuss? What are the
types?

2. Which sentence in the introductory paragraph names the types? Which
sentence or sentences in the concluding paragraph names them?

3. What are examples of holidays with pagan origins?

4. What are examples of patriotic holidays that the writer mentions?

---

[5]**fasting:** not eating or drinking; [6]**resurrection:** arising from death

Restrictive and Nonrestrictive Appositives

> **Appositives** are nouns or noun phrases that refer to the same person or thing as a preceding noun in a sentence.

Appositives can be **restrictive** (necessary) or **nonrestrictive** (unnecessary). Consider this sentence:

> My friend Tim got married last week.

In this sentence, *Tim* is an appositive because *Tim* and *my friend* are the same person. *Tim* is a restrictive (necessary) appositive because it is necessary to identify which friend got married. If we omit the word *Tim*, we don't know which friend got married.

On the other hand, consider this sentence:

> Tim, my friend, got married last week.

In this sentence, the appositive is *my friend*. It is nonrestrictive (unnecessary) because the name *Tim* already identifies the person who got married. If we omit *my friend*, we still know who got married. The fact that he is the writer's friend is not necessary to identify him. It is merely extra information.

If there is only one of an item that is referred to in a sentence, it is unnecessary to identify it further, so appositives of one-of-a-kind items are always nonrestrictive. For example, Earth has only one moon, so any appositive of *the moon* in a sentence would be nonrestrictive. Similarly, adjectives such as *tallest, strongest, oldest, most interesting* automatically make the following noun one of a kind.

> My son Carlos looks just like me. (Because there is more than one son, *Carlos* is necessary to identify which one the writer means. *Carlos* is a restrictive appositive.)
>
> My youngest son, Javier, looks just like his father. (Because there is only one youngest son, *Javier* is not necessary here. It is a nonrestrictive appositive.)

Here are two examples of appositives from the model essay. Can you explain why the first example needs a comma and the second one doesn't?

> A very clear example of a modern holiday with pagan origins is No Rooz, Iranian New Year.
>
> People in the United States have a holiday in February to celebrate the birthdays of the two great presidents George Washington and Abraham Lincoln.

COMMA RULE

Commas are used to separate nonrestrictive (unnecessary) appositives from the rest of the sentence. Commas are not used with restrictive (necessary) appositives.

PRACTICE:
Commas with Restrictive and Nonrestrictive Appositives

A. Locate and underline two or more appositives in the model essay on pages 151–152. Explain the use of commas in each one.

B. Underline the appositive in each of the following sentences. Then decide whether it is necessary or unnecessary and write *necessary* or *unnecessary* in the parentheses following each sentence. Finally, add commas to separate an unnecessary appositive from the rest of the sentence.

1. The planet Pluto is over two and a half billion miles from Earth.
(_____necessary_____).

2. Pluto, the most distant planet from Earth, is over two and a half billion miles away. (_____unnecessary_____)

3. Venus the closest planet to Earth is only twenty-five million miles away.
(_____)

4. The largest planet in the universe Jupiter is eleven times larger than Earth. (_____)

5. The moon is Earth's only satellite, but the planet Saturn has at least twenty-two satellites. (_____)

6. Astronomers scientists who study the stars believe that there is another planet in our solar system. (_____)

7. The terrible disease AIDS has killed hundreds of thousands of people.
(_____)

8. Governments are spending millions of dollars to combat AIDS a fatal illness.
(_____)

9. The world was shocked when basketball star Magic Johnson announced he was HIV-positive. (_____)

C. Write pairs of sentences containing appositives on your own. In one sentence, make the appositive unnecessary (nonrestrictive). In the other sentence, make it necessary (restrictive). Underline the appositives and add commas if necessary. You may write about holidays in your country or about any other topic.

1. a. <u>Christmas, a Christian holiday, is celebrated in many different ways.</u>

b. <u>The Christian holiday Christmas is celebrated in many different ways.</u>

2. a. _____

_____

b. _____

_____

3. a. _____

_____

b. _____

_____

4. a. _____

_____

b. _____

_____

Restrictive and Nonrestrictive Adjective Clauses

> **Adjective clauses** are clauses that modify nouns.

Adjective clauses begin with the words *who, whom, which,* and sometimes *that,* among others. You will learn how to write them in the next section. In this section, you will learn when to use commas with them.

Adjectives clauses can be restrictive or nonrestrictive, just as appositives can. Use the same comma rule:

- restrictive (necessary): no commas
- nonrestrictive (unnecessary): use commas to separate the adjective clause from the rest of the sentence.

Look at this sentence:

> Every culture in the world has special days that people observe with traditional food, customs, and events.

In this sentence, the clause *that people observe with traditional food, customs, and events* is an adjective clause that modifies the noun *days.* Since it is necessary to identify which days the writer is discussing, the clause is restrictive and commas are not used. *That* always introduces a restrictive clause.

Now read this sentence:

> Another example of a modern holiday with pagan origins is American Halloween, which is on October 31.

In this sentence, the clause *which is on October 31* is an adjective clause that modifies the noun *Halloween.* The clause is unnecessary to identify Halloween; it merely gives extra information about it. Therefore, commas are used to separate the clause from the rest of the sentence. *Which, who,* and *whom* introduce nonrestrictive clauses.

Underline the adjective clauses in the following sentences and draw an arrow to the noun each one modifies. Then decide whether each one is necessary or unnecessary, and write the words *necessary* or *unnecessary* in the parentheses following each sentence. Finally, add commas if they are needed.

Easter

PRACTICE:
Commas with Restrictive and Nonrestrictive Adjective Clauses

1. Some of the customs of Easter, which is a Christian holiday, have pagan origins. (___unnecessary.___)

2. People in northern and central Europe worshiped a goddess whom they called Eostre. (_____)

3. Eostre which means east was the goddess of spring. (_____)

4. Every spring, people who worshipped her held a festival to give thanks for the return of the sun's warmth. (_____)

5. They offered the goddess special cakes that they had baked for the festival. (_____)

6. These cakes were very similar to the hot cross buns that we have today at Easter. (_____)

7. Also, the custom of coloring eggs which families do at Easter came from ancient cultures. (_____)

8. Even the popular Easter bunny who brings chocolate eggs and other candy to children on Easter Sunday has pagan roots. (_____)

9. From these examples, we can see that Easter which is a Christian holiday that celebrates the resurrection of Jesus is mixed with many pagan customs that celebrate the arrival of spring. (_____)

   (_____) (_____)

Change small letters to capitals and add commas where appropriate in the following paragraphs.

april fool's day

a special day that many people enjoy is april fool's day which is celebrated on the first day of april in some countries. it is a day when people play tricks[1] on one another. people who don't remember what day it is may have a lot of surprises. my twin brother who loves to play tricks on his friends spends weeks thinking up new tricks for this special day.

no one knows when april fool's day began but some people believe it started in india long ago. in that country people still celebrate a spring holiday called holi. people fill bamboo[2] pipes with colored powder and blow them at passersby.[3] anyone who is outside may come home at the end of the day looking like a rainbow!

PART 3 Sentence Structure

*Complex
Sentences
with Adjective
Clauses*

In this section, you will learn how to write complex sentences with adjective clauses. You may remember from the preceding section that adjective clauses are clauses that modify nouns.

Look at this sentence:

Easter, which is a Christian holiday, is named for a pagan goddess.

The clause "which is a Christian holiday" is an adjective clause that modifies the noun *Easter*.

---

[1]**trick:** joke; [2]**bamboo:** kind of woody grass that has a hard, hollow stem; [3]**passersby:** people walking by (singular: passerby)

Here are some basic rules for adjective clauses.

---

1. Adjective clauses begin with the words *who*, *whom*, and *which*, among others. (relative pronouns)

2. In restrictive clauses only, use the relative pronoun *that* in place of *who* and *which*.

3. Adjective clauses are dependent clauses. You must join them to an independent clause to make a complex sentence.

4. Adjective clauses are placed in a sentence right after the noun they describe.

5. Non-restrictive adjective clauses are separated from the rest of the sentence by commas.

The correct relative pronoun to use depends on whether the clause is restrictive or nonrestrictive and on whether the relative pronoun is the subject or an object of its clause. You will learn about each of these types in the next sections.

Subject Pattern Adjective Clauses

When a relative pronoun is the subject of an adjective clause, the clause is a subject pattern adjective clause. You form subject pattern adjective clauses by changing the subject of a sentence to who (for people), which (for animals and things), or that (for people, animals, or things in restrictive clauses).

Look at these three sentences:

> Easter is a Christian holiday.
> Saint Valentine was an early Christian holy man.
> Easter and Christmas have pagan elements

We can turn these three sentences into dependent adjective clauses. Then we can add them to independent clauses to make complex sentences as follows:

Independent clause:	Easter is named for a pagan goddess.
Dependent adjective clause:	~~Easter~~ *which* is a Christian holiday.
Complex sentence:	Easter, which is a Christian holiday, is named for a pagan goddess.

Independent clause:	Valentine's Day is named for Saint Valentine.
Dependent adjective clause:	~~Saint Valentine~~ *who* was an early Christian holy man.
Complex sentence:	Valentine's Day is named for Saint Valentine, who was an early Christian holy man.

Independent clause:	Easter and Christmas are Christian holidays.
Dependent adjective clause:	~~Easter and Christmas~~ *that* have pagan elements.
Complex sentence:	Easter and Christmas are Christian holidays that have pagan elements.

PRACTICE:
Subject Pattern
Adjective Clauses

A. Make an adjective clause from the sentence in parentheses in each of the following pairs. Write it in the space provided to make a complete complex sentence. Add commas if they are needed.

1. Many religions have rules about food <u>that were developed for health</u>

   <u>reasons</u> . (The rules were developed for health reasons.)

2. Judaism _____

   has very strict rules about food. (Judaism is the oldest major religion in the world.)

3. Christians _____

   do not eat certain foods during the six weeks before Easter. (Some Christians practice fasting.)

4. People _____

   cannot eat beef. (People practice the Hindu religion.)

5. Moslems and Jews cannot eat pork _____

   _____ . (Pork is considered unclean.)

6. Moslems cannot eat or drink at all in the daytime during Ramadan _____

   _____ . (Ramadan is a holy month of fasting.)

B. Combine the sentences in each of the following pairs by making one of them an adjective clause and joining it to the other sentence. Be careful to put the clause immediately after the noun it modifies. Add commas if they are needed.

1. Three of the world's major religions were started by men. The men were teachers.

   <u>Three of the world's major religions were started by men who</u>

   <u>were teachers.</u>

2. Gautama Siddhartha was born about five hundred years before Jesus. Gautama Siddhartha started Buddhism.

   _____

3. Christianity was started by Jesus Christ. Jesus Christ was born about five hundred years before Mohammed.

   _____

4. A religion is monotheistic. A religion has one God.

   _____

5. The Hindu and Shinto religions are polytheistic. The Hindu and Shinto religions have many gods.

   _____

Object Pattern Adjective Clauses

When the relative pronoun is an object in an adjective clause, the clause is called an **object pattern adjective clause.** You form object pattern adjective clauses by changing any object in a sentence to *whom* (for people), *which* (for animals and things), or *that* (for animals or things in restrictive clauses). It is also possible to omit the relative pronoun in the object pattern.

The object can be a direct object, indirect object, or object of a preposition.

> Santa Claus brings <u>toys</u> to children. (direct object)
> He brings <u>children</u> toys. **or** He brings toys to <u>children.</u> (indirect object)
> Santa travels in <u>a sleigh.</u>[1] (object of preposition)

We can turn these sentences into adjective clauses by changing the objects to *that* and putting these relative pronouns before the subject of the sentences. We can add each of these clauses to an independent clause to make a complete complex sentence as follows:

Independent clause:	Santa Claus works all year long making toys.
Dependent adjective clause:	which he brings ~~toys~~ to children.
Complex sentence:	Santa Claus works all year long making toys, which he brings to children.

Independent clause:	Eight reindeer pull the sleigh.
Dependent adjective clause:	that Santa travels in ~~a sleigh~~.
Complex sentence:	Eight reindeer pull the sleigh that Santa travels in.

Independent clause:	Santa makes children very happy.
Dependent adjective clause:	whom he brings toys to ~~children~~
Complex sentence:	Santa makes children whom he brings toys to very happy.

PRACTICE:
Object Pattern Adjective Clauses

A. Make an adjective clause from the sentence in parentheses in each of the following pairs. Write it in the space provided to make a complete complex sentence. Add commas if they are needed.

1. People in Thailand have a festival _____ .
   (They call the festival Loy Krathong, "Festival of the Floating Leaf Cups.")

2. The Thais float little boats _____ down a river in the evening. (They have made the little boats out of banana leaves, lotus, or paper.)

3. The boats _____ float down the river in the moonlight. (They have decorated the boats with lighted candles, incense, coins, and flowers.)

---

[1]**sleigh:** vehicle with skis instead of wheels for travel on snow

B. Combine the sentences in each of the following pairs by making one of them an adjective clause and joining it to the other sentence. Be careful to put the clause immediately after the noun it modifies. Add commas if they are needed.

(Pongal is a three-day festival that celebrates the rice harvest in southern India.)

1. On the first day of Pongal, families gather in the kitchen and boil a pot of new rice. They cook the new rice in milk.

2. Then they offer some of the sweet rice to the sun god. They thank the sun god for ripening the rice crop. (Use *whom.*)

3. The second day of Pongal is for the rain. They thank the rain for helping the rice to grow by bringing gifts to the temple. (Use *which.*)

4. A traditional Pongal gift is a clay horse. They paint in bright colors.

5. On the third day of Pongal, the farmers honor their cattle. They decorate the cattle with flowers and coins.

PRACTICE:
Adjective Clauses

Write sentences with adjective clauses on your own. Define each of the following words with a sentence that contains an adjective clause. Use the words in parentheses to build your definition. Look up the words you don't know in a dictionary. All of your sentences will be restrictive.

1. fortune teller (a person): <u>A fortune teller is a person who can see into</u>
   <u>the future.</u>

2. travel agent (a person): _____

3. unicorn (an animal): _____

4. mah-jongg (a game): _____

5. fork (a utensil): _____

6. chopsticks (utensils): _____

Now think up some words of your own to define.

7. _____

_____

8. _____

_____

9. _____

_____

10. _____

_____

Sentence Combining

Combine the sentences in each group in any logical way to make one sentence. Your final sentence may be simple, compound, or complex. Look for opportunities to make adjective clauses. You may add words, delete words, or change words, but you must not omit any information or change the meaning. Write your final copy as a paragraph.

The First Thanksgiving

1. A modern Thanksgiving is similar in many ways to the first Thanksgiving.
The first Thanksgiving took place almost four hundred years ago.
It took place in the English colony of Massachusetts.

2. In 1620, the Pilgrims arrived in Plymouth, Massachusetts.
The Pilgrims were a religious group from England.

3. The Pilgrims came to the New World.
Their religion was different from the main religion in England.
(use because)

4. The Pilgrims' first winter was very hard.
Almost half of the group died.

5. They died of hunger.
They died of cold.
They died of disease.

6. The Indians of Massachusetts helped them.
They did this during the next year.
(Put the time expression first.)

7. The Indians taught the newcomers how to hunt.
The Indians taught the newcomers how to grow corn.
The Indians taught the newcomers how to survive in the New World.

8. The next winter came.
The Pilgrims had enough food.

9. They were grateful.
They had a feast to give thanks.

10. They shared food with the Indians.
They shared friendship with the Indians.
They invited the Indians to the feast.
(Use whom.)

11. A modern Thanksgiving is similar in spirit to the first Thanksgiving.
The food is probably different.

12. Today Americans eat turkey.
The Pilgrims and Indians probably ate deer.

PART 4 The Writing Process

Now let's complete the writing process you began at the beginning of the unit. Write an essay discussing different types of television programs that students in your class watch. Follow these steps in order to write a good essay.

STEP 1:
Prewrite to Get Ideas

This is the step you completed at the beginning of the unit.

STEP 2:
Organize the Ideas

Prepare an outline using logical division as a method of organization. Write a thesis statement and a concluding statement, and outline the body paragraphs. Each body paragraph should give the following information about each different kind of program:

- What is the purpose of this kind of program? To entertain? To inform? To educate?
- What times of day are these programs shown?
- Are they broadcast on the national networks, on local stations, or on educational channels?
- Who is the intended audience for this kind of program?

Include names of specific programs to illustrate your points.

STEP 3:
Write the Rough Draft

Write ROUGH DRAFT at the top of your paper. Write a rough draft from your outline. Try to include some adjective clauses.

STEP 4:
Edit the Rough Draft

Edit the rough draft. Follow the editing procedure that you have used in previous chapters.

EDITING CHECKLIST

Writer's Questions	Peer Editor's Answers and Comments
FORMAT	
1. Is the format correct?	Check the title, indenting, margins, and double spacing.
ORGANIZATION	
2. Does the essay have an introduction, a body, and a conclusion?	How many paragraphs does the essay have? How many paragraphs are in the body?
Introduction **3.** Do the general statements • give background information?	How many general statements are there? Is this a funnel introduction? yes no
• attract the reader's attention?	Does it stimulate your interest in the topic? yes no
4. Does the thesis statement state a clearly focused main idea for the whole essay?	Copy the thesis statement here:
Body **5.** Does each body paragraph have • a clearly stated topic sentence with a main (controlling) idea?	Write the main idea for each body paragraph:
• good development with sufficient supporting details (facts, examples, and quotations?)	List one supporting detail from each body paragraph:
• unity (one idea per paragraph)?	Underline any sentences that break the unity.
• coherence (logical organization and transition words)?	List the transitions between each body paragraph:
Conclusion **6.** Does the conclusion • restate your thesis or summarize your main points?	What kind of conclusion does the essay have? (Check one.) _____ summary of the main points
• give your final thoughts on the subject of your essay?	_____ restatement of the thesis

GRAMMAR AND MECHANICS	
7. Are commas used where necessary?	Circle any comma errors. Add missing commas.
8. Are verb tenses used appropriately?	Check each verb for the appropriate tense. Circle any that you have questions about.
SENTENCE STRUCTURE	
9. Do all sentences contain at least one subject and one verb and express a complete thought?	Underline any sentences that you have questions about.
10. Does the essay contain a variety of sentence types?	What sentence type (simple, compound, or complex) does this writer use the most often?
11. Are adjective clauses used?	Underline all adjective clauses and check them for correctness.

STEP 5:
Write the Second Draft
Write SECOND DRAFT at the top of your paper. Write the second draft of your essay to hand in to your instructor.

STEP 6:
Write the Final Draft
After your instructor returns your essay, write a neat final copy to hand in for final evaluation. Write FINAL DRAFT at the top of your paper.

 Write an essay on any of the following topics. Use logical division to organize your ideas.

1. Kinds of automobile drivers/shoppers/customers/teachers

2. People's personalities are reflected in their hairstyles/in their clothing

3. People's personalities are reflected in the way they walk/in the way they eat

4. People's personalities are reflected in the kinds of pets they have/cars they drive/food they eat

Unit 8 Supporting an Opinion

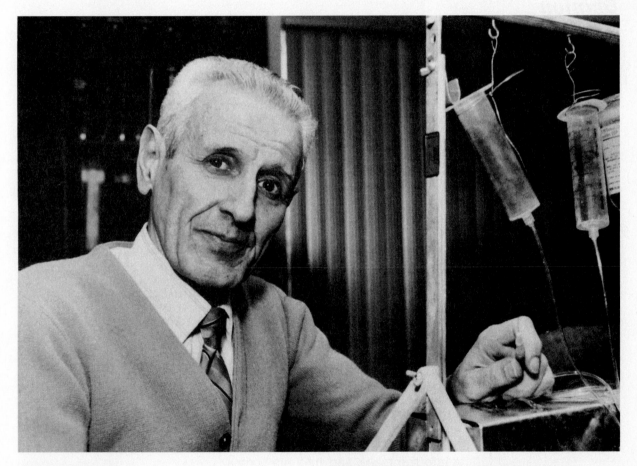

PREWRITING
- *Reading and Forming an Opinion*

ORGANIZATION
- *Opinion Essays*
- *Using Reasons to Support an Opinion*
- *Order of Importance*

  Transition Signals

GRAMMAR AND MECHANICS
- *Modal Verbs*

SENTENCE STRUCTURE
- *Reason Clauses*
- *Contrast Clauses*
- *Result Clauses*

THE WRITING PROCESS

*I*n Unit 7, you studied how to write essays using logical division of ideas that have something in common. In this unit, you will learn how to state an opinion about a subject that you agree or disagree with. You will also learn how to support your opinion with reasons by using facts and examples.

Prewriting: Reading and Forming an Opinion

Writers will often take a position on a controversial[1] issue that others will disagree with. As you read the model essays, you can form your own opinions. Work with a partner or a small group.

ACTIVITY

A. Read the following essay about the very controversial Dr. Jack Kevorkian.

The Suicide Doctor

Dr. Jack Kevorkian, a retired doctor, assists terminally ill[2] patients in committing suicide. Dr. Kevorkian strongly believes that physicians should be able to help terminally ill adults end their lives with self-respect, and his goal is to make assisted suicide legal.

5   Dr. Kevorkian invented a simple but effective machine that allows patients to take their own lives painlessly and efficiently. He provides the machine for his patients to commit suicide either by deadly injection or by carbon monoxide[3] poisoning. The patients cause their own death by pushing a button on the machine. For example, Dr.

10 Kevorkian hooked his first patient, Janet Adkins, up to the machine in 1990, and she pushed the button that released a deadly drug into her vein. Another patient was a fifty-three-year-old man who suffered from bone cancer. The patient wore a mask with a plastic tubing on his face. He caused his own death by removing the clip

15 from the plastic tubing. His action allowed the carbon monoxide to flow into the mask and into his body.

    Dr. Kevorkian has had his problems with the law. Michigan had no laws against assisted suicide when his first patient died in 1990. He was not accused of a crime but was ordered not to assist anyone

20 else in committing suicide. However, Dr. Kevorkian ignored the judge's order, and in 1991, he helped two more women, Mrs. Wantz and Mrs. Miller, end their lives. In 1992, he was charged[4] with murder in both of these deaths, but these charges were dismissed because the judge said that there was no evidence of murder.

---

[1]**controversial:** causing much argument or disagreement; [2]**terminally ill:** referring to people who are not expected to recover from their illness; [3]**carbon monoxide:** a poisonous gas (CO); [4]**charged:** accused of breaking the law

25   In April 1996, Dr. Kevorkian was put on trial[5] for the deaths of
Mrs. Wantz and Mrs. Miller. He was tried under Michigan's unwritten
common law[6] ruling that assisted suicide is a crime. The jury found
him not guilty and said that the doctor did not intend to kill the
women but was only trying to relieve their suffering. After he was
30   found not guilty, Dr. Kevorkian stated emphatically that he would not
stop helping terminally ill patients to end their lives with dignity.

   Although Dr. Kevorkian has had to face criminal charges and has
been criticized by both medical professionals and the media,[7] he still
remains a strong believer of death by choice. Moreover, he firmly
35   believes that he is only doing what he should do as a physician. It
will be interesting to see whether, in the future, the medical
profession and society as a whole will support Dr. Kevorkian in his
determination to continue his so-called "mission of mercy."[8]

B. Make notes of your opinions as you think about the answers to the following
   questions about Dr. Kevorkian.

   1. Do you think that Dr. Kevorkian really cares about ending the suffering
   of terminally ill people? Explain why you do or do not.

   2. Why do you think the doctor continues to help people end their lives?

   3. Why do you think the legal system cannot stop him from continuing
   his activities?

   4. How do you feel about Dr. Kevorkian and his activities? Is he a hero or
   an evil person?

   5. How would you advise someone who was terminally ill and feels
   hopeless enough to want to contact the doctor?

C. Decide whether you agree or disagree with Dr. Kevorkian and his work.

   1. Write a thesis statement in which you agree or disagree with
   Dr. Kevorkian and his work.

   Example: Dr. Kevorkian should not assist terminally ill patients in committing
   suicide for several reasons.

   2. Write an outline plan. Add supporting reasons for your opinion.

---

[5]**on trial:** having a formal examination of the facts of a case by a court of law; [6]**common
law:** law that comes from time-honored customs and court decisions; not a law passed
by the legislature; [7]**media:** newspapers, magazines, radio, television; [8]**mission of mercy:**
calling to action to relieve suffering

D. Discuss your point of view with your classmates. Try to convince them that your opinion is the right one. However, you may decide to change your position after your group discussion.

E. Save your outline plan and notes. You will use them later to write an essay.

MODEL ESSAY:
Supporting an Opinion

As you read the model essay, notice the opinion thesis statement and each reason that supports it.

The Right to Die

A difficult problem that is facing society is the legalization of euthanasia, another word for mercy killing. Euthanasia is a method of causing death painlessly to end suffering. People who are in a coma[1] because of accidents and elderly people who are terminally ill because of incurable[2] diseases are being
5 kept alive by artificial means. They do not have a chance to recover, but American laws do not allow doctors to end their lives. However, in my opinion, euthanasia should be legalized for several reasons.

The first and most important reason to support euthanasia is that these patients have no chance of recovery. They can never lead normal lives and
10 must be kept alive by life-support machines such as respirators to help them breathe and feeding tubes to provide them with nutrition.[3] They are clearly more dead than alive and will never be able to live a normal life. For example, after Samuel, an infant, had swallowed a balloon, he stopped breathing. The balloon was removed, but the lack of oxygen had caused brain damage and left
15 him in an irreversible[4] coma. Samuel was unable to breathe without the aid of a respirator, and there was no hope for his recovery.

Another reason to support mercy killing is that medical costs are very high. Today the cost of a hospital room can be as much as $1,450 per day for basic care, which does not include the cost of specialized care or the use of
20 special equipment. The high cost of medical care can cause financial problems for the family. For example, Charles Adkin's eighty-two-year-old wife lived in a nursing home in a coma for four years. Since there was no chance for her recovery, Mr. Adkins requested that the medical staff withhold treatment.

---

[1]**coma:** unconscious state (cannot see, hear, or speak); [2]**incurable:** cannot be made to go away by medical treatment; [3]**nutrition:** food; [4]**irreversible:** not changeable

25 However, his pleas were ignored. Soon after she died, Mr. Adkins was billed $250,000 for his wife's medical care. The courts ordered him to pay the bill, which must have placed a terrible financial burden[5] on him.

The final reason to support the legalization of euthanasia is that the family suffers. The nurses and other hospital staff can give the terminally ill patient only minimum care. Thus, the family must spend time to care for the special needs of

30 their loved one. For instance, Nancy Cruzan was kept alive on life-support machines for eight years. She would never recover from her vegetative[6] state. However, during those years, her loving, caring parents visited her regularly.

In the end, because terminally ill patients have no chance to recover and to live normal lives, they should be allowed to die with dignity. Therefore, the

35 family should have the right to ask doctors to turn off the life-support machines or to stop further medical treatment. To prolong life artificially when there is no hope for the future is a tragedy both for the patients and for their loved ones.

QUESTIONS ON THE MODEL

1. Which sentence expresses the writer's opinion about the right to die?

2. Underline the topic sentences that give reasons, and circle the transition signals.

3. What are the two parts of the conclusion?

4. Do you agree or disagree with the writer's final thought? Explain.

5. Do you think the nursing home should have listened to Mr. Adkin's request to withhold medical treatment from his wife? Explain.

PART 1 Organization

Opinion Essays

When you have an opinion and try to convince your listener or reader to accept your opinion, you are agreeing with or disagreeing with something. For example, in an everyday situation, you may try to convince a friend to have lunch or dinner at an Italian restaurant instead of at a Chinese one. Or you may try to talk someone into buying a red sports car instead of a blue one. In a college composition or speech class, the instructor may make an assignment in which

[5]**burden:** heavy responsibility; [6]**vegetative:** living like a plant, without mental activity

you must support or oppose the use of nuclear energy to produce electricity. In the business world, if you sell Triumph computers, you, of course, want your customers to buy your products instead of a competitor's. Therefore, you will try to convince your customers that your product and models are the best on the market. In any situation, if you strongly agree or disagree on an issue, you will want your reader or listener to accept your point of view.

Using Reasons to Support an Opinion

An **opinion** is what a person thinks about a subject. In the model essay, the writer says that people who cannot recover from their illnesses should have the right to die. That is the writer's opinion. She supports her opinion with several reasons.

Paragraph 2: The patients have no chance for recovery.
Paragraph 3: Medical costs are very high.
Paragraph 4: The family suffers.

Reread the second, third, and fourth paragraphs of the model composition. You will see that the writer has supported each of her reasons with facts and examples.

A **fact** is a true statement that can be proven. When you give your opinion about a subject, you want your reader to agree with you, so you must give reasons for your opinion. One of the ways to support your reasons is to give facts. Read the following examples:

Thesis Statement
Alcoholic beverages should be banned from college campuses for two reasons.

According to the controlling idea of the thesis statement, the writer is going to discuss two reasons why alcoholic beverages should not be allowed on college campuses.

Topic Sentence 1
The first reason is that drinking can cause academic failure.

Write the topic sentence as a question.

_____

Then answer the question to come up with a specific details to explain or support the topic sentence, as in the following model:

Main Supporting Ideas
–Unable to concentrate
–Miss classes, fail exams, and miss term paper deadlines

Supporting Facts and Examples
–My friend Dan
–Cypress College study

Here is the finished paragraph.

> Alcoholic beverages should be banned from college campuses for two reasons. *The first reason is that drinking can cause academic failure.* If students drink[1] before class or have a hangover[2] from drinking too much the night before, they will be unable to concentrate[3] on their school work. They may miss classes, fail exams, and miss term paper deadlines. This behavior could force them to drop out of school. For example, last semester, my friend Dan, who liked to party every night, dropped out of school. He failed organic chemistry twice and barely passed his other classes. As a result, his parents refused to pay for his education any longer. Recently, Cypress College did a study of student dropouts. Out of ninety cases reported, 65 percent dropped out because they had failing grades due to excessive[4] drinking. Therefore, it is true that drinking can interfere[5] with college success.

Topic Sentence 2
The second reason for banning alcoholic beverages from college campuses is that drinking and driving can be deadly.

Write the topic sentence as a question.

_____

Then answer that question to come up with specific details like in Topic Sentence 1.

PRACTICE:
Using Reasons to Support an Opinion

A. Work with a partner or a small group.

B. Brainstorm and discuss main supporting ideas and supporting facts and examples for topic sentence 2.

Main Supporting Idea 1 _____

_____

   Supporting Facts and Examples: _____

   _____

   _____

Main Supporting Idea 2 _____

_____

   Supporting Facts and Examples: _____

   _____

   _____

C. Write the second paragraph of the essay.

---

[1]**drink:** drink alcohol; [2]**hangover:** headache: sickness the day after drinking too much alcohol; [3]**concentrate:** keep all of one's thoughts, attention, or effort; [4]**excessive:** too much; [5]**interfere:** get in the way of

Order of Importance

Refer to the model essay on pages 170–171.

The first paragraph of the model essay is the introduction. It starts with several general statements and ends with the thesis statement:

> However, terminally ill patients should be allowed to end their lives by euthanasia for several reasons.

The body of the essay discusses three reasons, and it discusses them in the order of their importance (in the opinion of the writer). The most important reason is discussed first, and the least important is discussed last. Writers often use this order. On the other hand, it is also effective to begin with the least important reason and build up to the most important one at the end.

You can use either order in writing an opinion essay. Just be sure you put your arguments in order of importance, either beginning or ending with the most important argument.

Transition Signals

We know which reason the writer of the model essay thinks is the most important one because of the transition phrase she has used in the topic sentence: "The first and most important reason. . . ." It is necessary to tell the reader in what order you are discussing your ideas by using transition expressions that signal the order of things. The same transition expressions are used for time order and order of importance.

> The first (second, third) reason is . . .
> The first and most important reason is . . .
> The second reason is . . .
> Another reason is . . .
> The final reason is . . .

Of course, if you discuss your most important reason last, your transition expression should be the following:

> The final and most important reason is . . .

The concluding paragraph of an opinion essay is similar to any other conclusion:

- It ends the essay. (You may use a conclusion transition signal.)
- It summarizes the main reasons (or restates the thesis statement in different words).
- It may give the writer's final comment on the topic.

PRACTICE:
Transition Signals

Review the model essay on pages 170–171. Does the conclusion give a summary of the main reasons, or does it simply restate the thesis statement? What is the author's final comments? What conclusion transition expression does the author use? Circle all of the other transition signals you find in the essay. Explain their meanings.

WRITING PRACTICE:

Supporting Your Opinion

- Choose one opinion (**a** or **b**) from each of the following pairs of thesis statements.

- Brainstorm for reasons to support your thesis statement. Write down as many reasons as you can think of. Then choose two of the best reasons from your brainstorming list to support each thesis statement. Write each of these reasons as a topic sentence.

- Write down topic sentence 1. Brainstorm for specific details that will support it. You may ask yourself specific questions as the writer has done in the model paragraph. The answers to these questions will help you to develop your paragraph to support the topic sentence. Follow this step for both paragraphs.

- Remember to use sufficient specific details such as facts and examples to support each topic sentence.

1. **a.** It is a good idea for students to work part-time while they are going to school.

   b. Students should not work while they are going to school.

2. **a.** Young people should continue to live with their parents after they finish their education.

   b. Young people should move away from home after they finish their education.

3. **a.** Physical education courses should be required in college.

   b. Physical education courses should not be required in college.

4. **a.** Women can successfully mix motherhood and careers.

   b. Women should not work if they have young children.

PART 2 Grammar and Mechanics

MODEL ESSAY:
Modal Verbs

As you read the short model essay, notice the modal verbs.

Medical Marijuana[1]

Medical scientists and doctors in the United States have recently discovered that marijuana, an illegal drug, is an effective medicine for severely ill patients who cannot get relief from their usual prescription drugs. In my opinion, marijuana should be legal for medical uses because it can improve the quality of life for some people with serious illnesses.

5

(continued on the next page)

---

[1]**marijuana:** drug made from the dried flowers and leaves of the hemp plant; also called *grass, weed,* and *pot*

First of all, marijuana can help cancer patients who must undergo chemotherapy[1] or take anticancer drugs that cause serious side effects.[2] It can also help AIDS patients to regain their appetite and therefore to gain weight. Moreover, it might effectively stop the spread of glaucoma, which can cause

10   blindness, and it can relieve joint[3] pain and relax muscles in certain other illnesses. Unfortunately, because marijuana is an illegal drug, it cannot be purchased even with a doctor's prescription at a pharmacy.

In brief, smoking marijuana is effective enough to help seriously ill people enjoy a meal or live without constant pain. Therefore, marijuana for medical

15   purposes should be legal.

QUESTIONS ON THE MODEL

1. What is the writer's opinion about legalizing marijuana for medical uses?

2. Underline the opinion statement.

3. Name several of the illnesses that can be relieved by smoking marijuana.

4. Why can't patients buy marijuana at a pharmacy?

5. Circle all verbs with modals and explain their meanings. (Use the chart on page 177.)

6. Underline all of the transition signals in the model and be able to explain their meanings.

Modal Verbs

Modal verbs are words that add special meaning—possibility, necessity, permission, and so on—to the main verbs that follow them.

Modals include *can, could, will, would, shall, should, ought to, must, have to, may* and *might*.

Modals have two forms: present and past, but the form of the modal does not necessarily express time in the sentence. Modals are *always* used with the simple form of the verb.

> Gerry might be a witness. (present or future)
> He should tell the truth. (present)
> You can/could attend the trial. (future)

---

[1]**chemotherapy:** use of chemical agents to treat a disease; [2]**side effects:** secondary reactions, results; [3]**joint:** place where bones connect

MODAL VERBS

Modal	Usage	Negative Form Contraction
can	**expresses ability or inability and possibility or impossibility** Euthanasia can end life painlessly. (ability) People on life-support machines can't breathe or eat on their own. (inability) Life-support machines can prolong life. (possibility) Patients on life-support machines cannot ever live a normal life	cannot can't
could	**expresses possibility or impossibility** Doctors could pull the plug. (possibility) Samuel couldn't survive without the respirator. (impossibility)	could not couldn't
may/might	**expresses weak possibility** You may/might get a prescription from your doctor. However, the pharmacy may not/might not fill it for you.	may not might not
should ought to	**express advice** The courts should legalize euthanasia. The courts ought to allow euthanasia. Dr. Kevorkian shouldn't aid terminally ill patients in committing suicide.	should not shouldn't
must have to	**express necessity or lack of necessity** The family must respect the patient's final wishes. (necessity) They have to discuss it with the doctor. (necessity) The family must not forget the patient's final wishes. (negative necessity) The family doesn't have to make the final decision about euthanasia alone. (lack of necessity)	must not mustn't does/do not have to doesn't/don't have to
will	**expresses future action** Lowering the drinking age to eighteen will cause problems. Which state will not raise its legal drinking age to twenty-one?	will not won't

A. Add a modal and a main verb to the following sentences. The meaning of the modal you should use is given in parentheses after each sentence. Choose an appropriate main verb from the following list, and use it only once: *prevent, drop, show, lose, keep, find, check, forfeit, get, enter.*

1. The national minimum drinking age in the United States ___should remain___ at 21. (advice)

2. States _____ the minimum age for drinking at 21. (necessity)

3. The legal drinking age _____ from 21 to 18. (negative necessity)

4. Otherwise, the states _____ federal money to build highways. (possibility)

5. Raising the drinking age _____ teenagers from drinking. (weak impossibility)

6. Teenagers _____ it more difficult to buy alcohol. (future action)

7. Young people _____ identification cards to prove that they are old enough to drink. (necessity)

8. Without ID cards, teenagers _____ a bar. (impossibility)

9. Bartenders _____ ID cards carefully. (necessity)

10. Last week, 18-year-old Janet _____ into a bar with her 21-year-old boyfriend. (past impossibility)

11. A bar _____ its legal permit to sell liquor if it sells alcoholic beverages to teenagers. (possibility)

B. Complete the following essay with the best modals from this list: *can, could, may/might, should/ought to, must/have to, will.* Also, use negative modal forms and contractions where it is possible.

Women in the Military

Today American women ____can____ choose a career in a branch of
                          1.

the armed forces. They _____ take advantage of opportunities to
                          2.

pursue[1] an exciting career and educational goals. They are given most

---

[1]**pursue:** undertake, seek

of the same opportunities as men in uniform such as flying planes or helicopters; however, they _____ go into armed combat.[2] I agree
3.
with this policy. In my opinion, women _____ fight in wars for
4.
several reasons.

The first and most important reason why women _____ fight
5.
in combat is because of their role in life. Since they bring new life into the world by giving birth, it _____ be difficult for them to
6.
take a life. However, in combat, they _____ make an instant
7.
decision to kill or be killed. Any hesitation _____ result in their
8.
death or the death of other soldiers fighting with them.

Another reason why women _____ fight is because they do
9.
not have the physical strength that men have. In hand-to-hand combat with an enemy, they _____ be able to defend themselves.
10.
Therefore, once again, they _____ endanger not only their own
11.
lives but also the other soldiers' lives.

The final reason for banning women from actual combat is the problems that _____ arise between the sexes. For example, men
12.
_____ have confidence fighting alongside women. Moreover, the
13.
men _____ worry about the women's safety. These situations
14.
_____ make it more difficult to win a conflict against the enemy
15.
on land, on the sea, or in the air.

In short, women in the military _____ go into direct combat.
16.
They _____ be very effective in helping their country in non-
17.
combat support jobs. Therefore, women _____ accept the policy
18.
that prevents them from fighting in wars.

---

[2]**combat:** fighting

WRITING PRACTICE: *Modal Verbs*

Work with a small group. Read about the problems of the Jones family, which are explained below. Discuss the family's problems with your group and the action that the family *should* take, *ought to* take, *might* take, *can* take, *could* take, *must* take, or *have to* take. What *shouldn't* they do? What *mustn't* they do? What *can't* they do? Then write a letter giving advice to the Joneses.

- Begin your letter as follows:

  Dear Mr. and Mrs. Jones,

  I am sorry to hear about your problems, and I would like to offer you some

  advice. I think you ought to _____ . Of course, you can always

  _____ . You certainly must _____ , but you shouldn't _____ .

- Use as many different modals as fit the meaning. Include some negative modals, too.
- With a partner, edit and revise your letter. Check your own and your partner's letters for the appropriate use of modal verbs.

The Jones Family

Mr. and Mrs. Jones have a family problem. They have one son, whose name is Tom. They have no other children. Tom is a high school senior and will go to college next year. He is an excellent student and a good son. He is rather quiet, and he has few friends. His parents both work in the successful family furniture business that they started themselves twenty years ago. The business has grown from no employees to forty-five employees. Mr. and Mrs. Jones work six days a week, and Tom helps them whenever they ask him to.

Tom has one passion[1] in life: music. He wants to study music in college and hopes to become a professional musician. He plays the violin well, and he has been offered a scholarship to study music at a top-rated music school in New York City. His parents, however, want him to study business so that he can take over the family business and they can retire. Tom hates business. He cares about making music, not about making money.

---

[1]**passion:** very strong interest

PART 3 Sentence Structure

Three kinds of clauses are useful when you write an opinion essay: reason, contrast, and result clauses. The following chart lists the transition signals that introduce these kinds of clauses. The transition signals are classified into three groups: sentence connectors, coordinators, and subordinators.

Transition Signals

Kind of Clause	Sentence Connectors	Coordinators	Subordinators
Reason (to give reasons)			because since as
Contrast (to add opposite ideas)	however nevertheless	but	even though although
Result (to give results or effects)	therefore consequently	so	

Reason Clauses

Reason clauses answer the question "Why?"

Because, since, and *as* are subordinators that introduce dependent reason clauses. They give the reason for the idea in the independent clause. The reason clause can come before or after the independent clause.

Example: Volcanoes are always dangerous. (statement)
Why are volcanoes always dangerous?
. . . because they give no warning signals. (reason)
Volcanoes are always dangerous because they give no warning signals.
Because volcanoes give no warning signals, they are always dangerous.

Remember the comma rule: If the dependent clause comes at the beginning of a sentence, use a comma.

A. Read each of the following pairs of sentences carefully. Choose the clause that gives the reason for the other clause. Then add a subordinator to the reason clause and write a new sentence by combining the reason clause with the independent clause. Use correct punctuation.

NOTE: When the subject (or objects) of both clauses are the same, use a noun in the first clause and a pronoun in the second clause.

1. Pollution is a problem.
   Pollution affects our health. (reason)

   Pollution is a problem because it affects our health.

   or

   Because pollution affects our health, it is a problem.

2. Noise is a form of pollution.
   Noise can damage our health.

   _____

   _____

3. Noise is harmful to the body.
   Noise can change the heart rate and increase blood pressure.

   _____

   _____

4. The mother's body reacts to noise.
   Noise can affect an unborn baby.

   _____

   _____

5. The noise level near a school should not be high.
   Children need a quiet environment to learn in.

   _____

   _____

B. Complete the following sentences with a reason clause or an independent clause. Use correct punctuation.

1. Riding a bicycle is popular because *it is good exercise.*

   _____

2. Since bicycles are more economical than cars _____

_____

3. Because bicycling is a good exercise _____

_____

4. Since _____
parking is not a problem.

5. Riding a bicycle is better than driving because _____

_____

C. Write four original sentences–two using the reason subordinator *because* and two using *since*.

Contrast Clauses

> **Contrast clauses** are independent or dependent clauses that present an idea that contrasts with another idea in the sentence.

However and *nevertheless* are sentence connectors that introduce contrast clauses. They connect the idea in the first clause with a contrasting idea in the second clause. These sentence connectors tell the reader that an opposite idea from the first clause will follow. *However* and *nevertheless* should be followed by a comma. (Review the punctuation of sentence connectors on page 91.)

Example: A motorcycle is fun to ride. (statement)
A motorcycle can be dangerous. (contrasting or opposite idea)
A motorcycle is fun to ride; however, it can be dangerous.

PRACTICE:
Contrast Clauses, Part 1

A. Read each of the following pairs of sentences carefully. Write the clause that would best begin the sentence. Then add a sentence connector and write the second clause. Use correct punctuation.

1. A secondhand[1] one is reasonable.
The cost of a new motorcycle is high.

_____

_____

2. Young people don't worry about that.
A motorcycle doesn't protect the rider.

_____

_____

―――――――――――
[1]**secondhand:** not new

(continued on the next page)

3. Motorcyclists should wear helmets.[1]
    Many of them don't like to wear them.

    _____

    _____

4. My parents won't let me buy one.
    I want to buy a motorcycle.

    _____

    _____

5. I also want a motorcycle.
    I own a sports car.

    _____

    _____

B. Write four original sentences—two using the sentence connector *however* and two using *nevertheless*.

Although and *even though* are subordinators that introduce a dependent clause showing a contrast to the idea in the independent clause. They have the same meaning as the sentence connectors *however* and *nevertheless*.

The *although* or *even though* clause can come at the beginning of the sentence or after the independent clause.

Example: Although I should buy a car, I want to buy a motorcycle.
I want to buy a motorcycle although I should buy a car.

_____

[1]**helmet:** hard hat to protect the head

PRACTICE:
*Contrast Clauses,
Part 2*

A. Rewrite the sentences in the practice part 1 on pages 183–184 using the subordinators *although* and *even though*. You may place the contrast clause either before or after the independent clause. Notice the punctuation.

1. _Although the cost of a new motorcycle is high,_ a secondhand one is reasonable.

   or

   A secondhand motorcycle is reasonable _even though the cost of a new_ _one is high._

2. _____

   _____

3. _____

   _____

4. _____

   _____

5. _____

   _____

B. Write four original sentences—two using the subordinator *although* and two using *even though*.

Result Clauses

> **Result clauses** are independent clauses that tell the result of something described in the first independent clause.

Therefore and *consequently* are sentence connectors that connect two independent clauses when the second clause is the result of the first clause. They have the same meaning as the coordinator *so*. Both *therefore* and *consequently* should be followed by a comma.

Example: Marriage is back in style. (statement)
Many couples are taking the big step.[2] (result)
Marriage is back in style; therefore, many couples are taking the big step.

---

[2]**taking the big step:** making a big decision (idiom)

PRACTICE:
Result Clauses

A. Read each of the following pairs of sentences carefully. Choose the clause that gives the result. Then combine the sentences, and add *therefore* or *consequently* before the result clause. Punctuate the sentences correctly.

1. Marriage is not easy.
   A couple should work hard to make it successful.

   _____

   _____

2. Their husbands should help with the housework.
   Many women continue to work after marriage.

   _____

   _____

3. Many married women earn high salaries.
   Their husbands don't have to worry about paying all the bills.

   _____

   _____

4. Some married women take care of all the housework and cooking.
   Some married women don't work outside the home.

   _____

   _____

5. Many young couples have unrealistic[1] ideas about marriage.
   Many marriages end in divorce.

   _____

   _____

B. Complete the following sentences using the sentence connectors *consequently* or *therefore*. Choose the best clause from the following list to complete each sentence on the next page. Use correct punctuation.

I can speak with Americans better	I have a lot more confidence
We had a lot of practice	The teacher tried to help us
My friends didn't understand me before	We all had to speak English
We were nervous	We weren't nervous

---

[1]**unrealistic:** impractical; unreasonable

1. Last semester I took an English conversation class; _therefore, I can speak_
    with Americans better. _____

    _____

2. We had to speak English all the time _____

    _____

3. The teacher told us not to worry about our mistakes _____

    _____

4. My classmates were from many countries of the world _____

    _____

5. We couldn't pronounce the "th" sounds like in "thank" and "think"

    _____

PRACTICE:
*Sentence
Completion*
Complete the following sentences with your own ideas. Use correct punctuation.

1. I want to travel around the world; however, _I don't have the time_
    or money. _____

2. I don't have the money therefore _____

    _____

3. My friends are going to Paris and London nevertheless _____

    _____

4. I would like to go because _____

    _____

5. Even though traveling is expensive _____

    _____

6. Since traveling is educational _____

    _____

PART 4 The Writing Process

Now let's complete the writing process you began at the beginning of the unit. Write an opinion essay about whether you agree or disagree with Dr. Kevorkian and his work. You have already completed steps 1 and 2 in the writing process. Continue the process with Step 3.

STEP 3:
Write the Rough Draft

Write ROUGH DRAFT at the top of your paper. Follow your outline, and write a rough draft.

- Use order of importance to organize your reasons.

- Use a variety of sentence structures. Use sentence connectors, coordinating conjunctions, and subordinating conjunctions to vary your sentences.

STEP 4:
Edit the Rough Draft

Edit the rough draft. Follow the editing procedure you used in previous units.

EDITING CHECKLIST

Writer's Questions	Peer Editor's Answers and Comments
FORMAT	
1. Is the format correct?	Check the title, indenting, margins, and double spacing.
ORGANIZATION	
2. Does the essay have an introduction, a body, and a conclusion?	How many paragraphs does the essay have? How many paragraphs are in the body?
Introduction 3. Do the general statements • give background information? • attract the reader's attention?	How many general statements are there? Is this a funnel introduction? yes no Does it stimulate your interest in the topic? yes no
4. Does the thesis statement state a clearly focused main idea for the whole essay?	Copy the thesis statement here:
Body 5. Does each body paragraph have • a topic sentence that states a reason • good development with sufficient supporting details (facts, examples, and quotations)?	 Write the main idea for each body paragraph: List one supporting detail from each body paragraph.

ORGANIZATION (continued)	
• unity (one idea per paragraph)?	Underline any sentences that break the unity.
• coherence (logical organization and transition words)?	List the transitions between each body paragraph:
• Is order of importance used to organize the body paragraphs?	yes no
Conclusion **6.** Does the conclusion	What kind of conclusion does the essay have?
• restate your thesis or summarize your main points?	(Check one.) ____ summary of the main points
• give your final thoughts on the subject of your essay?	____ restatement of the thesis
GRAMMAR AND MECHANICS	
7. Are modal verbs used appropriately and correctly?	Check each verb. Circle any errors.
SENTENCE STRUCTURE	
8. Does the essay contain a variety of sentence types?	What sentence type does this writer use the most often? Circle one: simple compound complex
9. Are structure words for reason, contrast, and result clauses varied?	List some reason, contrast, and result structure words used.

STEP 5:
Write the Second Draft

Write SECOND DRAFT at the top of your paper. Write the second draft of your essay to hand in to your instructor.

STEP 6:
Write the Final Draft

After your instructor returns your essay, write a neat final copy to hand in for final evaluation. Write FINAL DRAFT at the top of your paper.

ADDITIONAL WRITING

Here are additional topics for opinion essays. Choose only one position to write about. Do not discuss both sides of the topic.

1. Ordinary citizens should/should not be allowed to own handguns.

2. The legal drinking age in the United States should/should not be lowered from twenty-one to eighteen.

3. The legal drinking age in the United States should/should not be abolished.[1]

4. Communities should/should not have an 11:00 P.M. curfew[2] for teenagers.

---

[1]**abolished:** gotten rid of, canceled; [2]**curfew:** specific time when people must be indoors

Unit 9 Comparison-Contrast

*I*n this unit, you will learn how to write about similarities and differences. To start thinking about similarities and differences between two cultures, do Activity 1 or 2 as your teacher directs. For these activities, you will have to get information about another culture. You may get this information from an ESL classmate, or you may talk to an American to get information about American culture.

Prewriting: Interviewing

Fill in the chart with information about elementary or secondary educational systems in your country and in another country. You may use the United States or another country as the "other country" in the chart.

ACTIVITY 1   **EDUCATIONAL SYSTEMS**   My Country: Other Country:

_____   _____

Time Spent in School		
How many years are students required to attend school?		
How are these years divided?		
How many hours per day are students at school? How many days per week?		
How many weeks of vacation are there? When are the vacations?		
Curriculum[1]		
What academic subjects do students study in elementary school? In high school? What nonacademic subjects do they take (music, art, etc.)?		
How many hours of homework do students have each night or each week?		
Is there a different teacher for each subject?		
Do students have to take exams to pass into the next grade? When do they take exams?		

---

[1]**curriculum:** course of study

Teachers and Teaching Styles		
Are the teachers mostly men or women?		
What kind of training do teachers have?		
What is the classroom atmosphere, formal or informal? Do students stand up when teachers enter the room? How do students behave? Do students sit at desks or at tables? How are they arranged in the room?		
How do teachers grade students? How do teachers reward or punish students?		
Do students discuss and ask questions, or do they just listen and answer questions asked by the teacher?		
Miscellaneous		
Do students wear uniforms?		
What extracurricular activities are there at school (clubs, sports teams, school plays, etc.)?		
Are parents active in the schools? How do parents participate?		
(Think of other questions of your own to ask.)		

ACTIVITY 2 Fill in the chart with information about family structure in your country and in another country. You may use the United States or another country as the "other country" in the chart.

FAMILY STRUCTURE   My Country: Other Country:

Roles of the Adults		
Who is the head of the family?		
Who controls the family's money?		
Who makes most of the decisions?		
Who raises the children? Who disciplines the children?		
Who does the everyday shopping? Who shops for large items such as a new car?		
Who does the cooking and cleaning?		
Do both parents work outside the home?		

FAMILY STRUCTURE　　　　**My Country:**　　**Other Country:**

Roles of the Children		
Are all children treated equally?		
Do all children have the same responsibilities?		
Do all children do chores at home?		
Do children receive a weekly allowance?		
At what age do children make their own decisions?		
At what age do children move out of their parents' house?		
General		
How many family members live in one house?		
Where do older relatives (grandparents, aunts, uncles) live? Who takes care of them?		
In general, how are parents treated by their children? How are children treated by their parents? How are grandparents treated by their children and grandchildren?		
(Think of other questions of your own to ask.)		

Save this information. You will use it at the end of the unit to write an essay.

MODEL ESSAY:

Comparison-Contrast

As you read the model essay, notice which paragraphs discuss differences and which paragraphs discuss similarities between school systems in Europe and the United States.

School Systems in Europe and the United States

A nation's purpose in educating its children is to prepare them to become productive members of society. Each country in the world has developed a system of education based on its needs, economic resources, and traditions. One would think that industrial societies such as the United States and the

---

(continued on the next page)

SOURCE: Delhaxhe, Arlette. "European Schools Offer Contrasts and Similarities," *The Christian Science Monitor*, September 8, 1993, p. 11.

5   countries of Europe would have similar systems for educating their children. However, a comparison of school systems in Europe and the United States reveals several similarities but a great number of differences.

The educational systems of Europe and the United States are similar in a number of ways. To begin with, elementary school classes look the same
10   everywhere: There are about twenty to twenty-two pupils per class, and the classes are coeducational.[1] Also, there is one teacher for all subjects for each grade (except in Scandinavia), and the majority of elementary school teachers are women. In addition, the subjects taught at the elementary level are basically the same everywhere: reading and writing, mathematics, introductions to the
15   sciences, music, sports, and art. The only major difference in the elementary curriculum is that most Europeans study a foreign language in elementary school, but most American children do not.

Second, European and American students spend approximately the same number of years in school. Both the United States and most European
20   countries require children to attend school for at least nine or ten years. Germany and Belgium have the highest requirement: twelve years of education. Also, children in most countries start compulsory[2] schooling at a similar age, usually age six, and they may leave school at a similar age, usually age sixteen.

Despite these similarities, the educational systems differ greatly in several
25   areas. For example, the number of hours per day and days per year that children must attend school varies widely. The number of hours students must spend per day in high school ranges from[3] a low of five in Belgium to a high of eight in parts of Hungary and Turkey. Some countries require a half-day of school, whereas others require a full day. In addition, the number of days per
30   year that students must be in school differs. Austria requires 237 days of school per year, while Spain and Hungary require only 170. That is a difference of more than two months!

Another major difference is in the types of schools available. In the countries of Northern Europe, there is no division between elementary and
35   secondary school; school just flows from the first day of first grade until the end of compulsory schooling at age sixteen. However, in the United States,

---

[1]**coeducational:** attended by both boys and girls; [2]**compulsory:** required;
[3]**ranges from . . . to:** starts at . . . and goes to

school is divided into nine years of elementary and four years of secondary education. Furthermore, some countries require students to make a choice between academic preparatory[4] and vocational training[5] schools. In Germany, pupils must make this decision as early as age ten. In the United States, in contrast, they never have to make it. Anyone in the United States who graduates from high school has the opportunity to go on to a college or university.

40

In addition to the differences in academic and vocational schools, there are also differences in private schools. In France, Spain, Belgium, and Austria, most private schools are religious, but in most other countries, they are not. Also, in most of Europe, the government pays part of the cost of private schools: 70 percent in Hungary, 80 percent in Denmark and Austria, and 85 percent in Norway. In contrast, parents must pay the full cost in Britain, Greece, Turkey, and the United States if they want their children to attend a private school.

45

A final major difference between Europe and the United States is in the number of students who go on to higher education.[6] In the United States, over 50 percent of high school graduates enter a college or university. In contrast, fewer than 15 percent of British students do so. The European average is about 30 to 40 percent.

50

It is clear that the experience of schoolchildren varies from country to country. Even though the United States and the countries of Europe seem very similar in many ways, their educational systems are actually quite different. No one can say if one system is better than another system, for each one fits its own needs, economies, and traditions the best.

55

QUESTIONS ON THE MODEL

1. What is the purpose of the first paragraph of the essay?

2. Underline the thesis statement. What does it tell you about the organization of the body paragraphs?

3. How many paragraphs are in the body of the essay? Which paragraphs discuss differences? Which discuss similarities?

4. Which are discussed first—the similarities or the differences? In which paragraph does the changeover occur? Underline the transition phrase that introduces the changeover.

---

[4]**academic preparatory school:** school that prepares students for college or university studies; [5]**vocational training school:** school that prepares students to work at an occupation; [6]**higher education:** college or university

PART *1* Organization

Comparison-Contrast Essays

Comparing and contrasting, or thinking about similarities and differences, is an activity that we do every day whenever we have to make decisions. When buying a new car, you compare and contrast several cars before choosing one. When thinking about what classes to take next semester, you compare and contrast the teachers and the class hours before making your choices. Even deciding where to eat involves comparing and contrasting.

We also frequently make comparisons and contrasts in writing. In the business world, you may have to evaluate proposals from two companies who want to do business with you, or you may have to evaluate two job applicants, two computer systems, or two health insurance plans. This chapter will show you how to do this.

Block Organization

A comparison and contrast essay can be organized in several ways. However in this book, you will learn the most basic pattern, which is called **block organization.**

In block organization, the similarities are discussed together in one block (which can be one paragraph or several paragraphs). Then the differences are discussed together in one block. As you can see from this outline, the model essay uses block organization. The two paragraphs of similarities are a block, and the four paragraphs of differences are a block.

School Systems in Europe and the United States

> I. Introduction
>   A. General statements
>   B. Thesis statement

> II. Similarities - elementary schools
>   A. Class size and composition
>   B. One teacher
>   C. Curriculum

> III. Similarities - years of compulsory education
>   A. Number of years
>   B. Ages

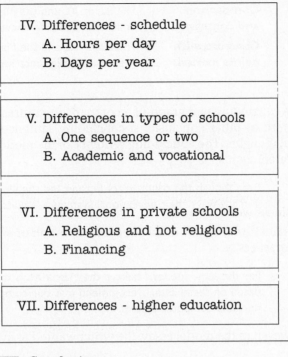

IV. Differences - schedule
  A. Hours per day
  B. Days per year

V. Differences in types of schools
  A. One sequence or two
  B. Academic and vocational

VI. Differences in private schools
  A. Religious and not religious
  B. Financing

VII. Differences - higher education

VIII. Conclusion
  A. Concluding sentence(s)
  B. Final thoughts

You may, of course, discuss the differences first and then the similarities.

Thesis Statements

The thesis statement in a comparison-contrast essay should clearly name the topics of the comparison. It should also indicate that this is going to be a comparison-contrast analysis. The thesis statement sometimes also names the points on which the topics are going to be compared and contrasted. Let's look at the thesis statement of the model essay.

> However, a comparison of school systems in Europe and the United States reveals several similarities but a great number of differences.

The topics are named:

> school systems in Europe and school systems in the United States

These words show that the essay will be a comparison-contrast analysis:

> a comparison of
> several similarities but a great number of differences

Here are some further examples of thesis statements for comparison and contrast. These sentences are about two car models.

Comparison only: The Super XL and the Magna XL are alike in several ways.

Contrast only: The Super XL and the Magna XL have some very important differences.

Comparison and contrast:	The Super XL and the Magna XL have both similarities and differences.
Contrast, with points named:	The Super XL and the Magna XL are different in exterior design, interior design, and comfort.

Concluding Paragraphs

The concluding paragraph of a comparison-contrast essay can follow the same pattern as other conclusions: concluding sentence(s) followed by the writer's final thoughts. The concluding sentence of the model essay restates the thesis in different words:

> Even though the countries of Europe and the United States seem very similar in many ways, their educational systems are quite different.

The final comment is often a recommendation or a judgment in a comparison-contrast essay:

> For the same money, I believe the Magna XL is the better car to buy.
> Based on these data, I recommend that our company buy the XYZ rather than the ABC computer system.

However, in the model essay, the writer wanted to avoid making a judgment:

> No one can say if one system is better than another system, for each one fits its own needs, economies, and traditions the best.

PRACTICE:
Organizing a Comparison-Contrast Topic

Work with a partner or a small group. You are a travel agent, and a wealthy client has asked you to help her decide on a vacation destination. She wants to go during the summer, and she is considering Alaska and Hawaii. Both places are popular tourist destinations. You have gathered some information about the two places. You now need to organize this information and prepare a written report.

1. Study the list of information about Alaska and Hawaii. Clarify any unfamiliar vocabulary.

2. The information is not in any order. Organize the information by filling in the chart. Begin by assigning the items to one of the following main topics:

Accommodations (hotels and restaurants)
Environment
Transportation
Climate
Natural Beauty

Then put the information in the appropriate boxes.

The ocean and rivers in Alaska are unpolluted.

There is no air pollution in Hawaii.

The temperature is perfect in Alaska during the summer.

The food in Alaska is poor in quality and expensive.

There is no humidity in Alaska.

Alaska has the Chugach Mountains and Mount McKinley, the highest mountain in North America.

There is a wide variety of excellent restaurants in Hawaii.

It is terribly humid in Hawaii in the summer.

Most people fly to Hawaii by jumbo jet.

Hawaii has Volcano National Park and Waimea Canyon.

It can be very hot in Hawaii in the summer.

The ocean surrounding Hawaii is clean, and the rivers are unpolluted.

The beaches in Hawaii are among the most beautiful in the world.

The glaciers in Alaska are awesome.

Hotels in Alaska are expensive, and their quality is generally poor.

The air in Alaska is pure and clean.

It often rains during the summer in Hawaii.

Most people travel to Alaska by cruise ship.

There is a wide range of excellent hotels in Hawaii, from luxury to budget priced.

It's impractical to rent a car in Alaska because the distances are too great.

Rental cars are cheap and convenient in Hawaii.

It seldom rains during the summer in Alaska.

	ALASKA	HAWAII
ACCOMMODATIONS		
ENVIRONMENT		
TRANSPORTATION		
CLIMATE		
NATURAL BEAUTY	Chugach Mountains and Mount McKinley	

3. Make a formal outline for your report. Your outline should have seven paragraphs. Include these in your outline:

> A thesis statement
> A conclusion (Make a recommendation to your client.)
> Paragraphs of similarities
> Paragraphs of differences
> Topic sentences for each paragraph

Use the outline on pages 196–197 as a model.

PART 2 Sentence Structure

MODEL ESSAY:

Comparison-Contrast Structure Words

As you read the model essay, look for words and phrases that show similarities and differences.

Gender[1] Differences

The "battle of the sexes" started with Adam and Eve,[2] and it will probably continue forever. The opinion that men are superior to women has long been accepted in many cultures, but the feminist movement[3] is trying to change this view. Feminists claim that boys and girls are exactly equal at birth but become
5 unequal because of the way they are treated by society. However, recent research contradicts[4] the view that males and females are innately[5] alike.

Without a doubt, societal influences both inside and outside the family cause many differences to develop. Inside the family, boys learn to be men by watching and copying their fathers, and girls learn to be women by watching
10 and copying their mothers. Outside the family, boys who play with dolls after a certain age receive disapproval, as do girls who continue to play with Ninja Turtles (although the pressure may not be quite as strong on girls).

However, not all differences are caused by societal influences. Some are due to differences in the physiology[6] of the brain. For example, more men than
15 women are left-handed, which means that the right side of men's brains are

---

[1]**gender:** sex; [2]**Adam and Eve:** the first man and woman, according to Judeo-Christian tradition; [3]**feminist movement:** activities and people in support of equality for women; [4]**contradicts:** says or proves that the opposite is true; [5]**innately:** by birth, naturally; [6]**physiology (of the brain):** functioning (of the brain)

dominant[7] because the right side of the brain controls the left side of the body. Right-brain people generally have better reasoning abilities, whereas left-brain people generally have better verbal skills.

20   In fact, girls are better at language than boys. For both men and women, the language center is on the left side of the brain. However, girls not only begin speaking earlier than boys, but they also speak more clearly and develop larger vocabularies. In contrast, more boys than girls stutter[8] and have trouble learning to read. Boys' difficulty with language may be the result of their right-brain dominance.

25   In addition, men and women have different spatial abilities. For example, men are better at turning three-dimensional[9] objects in their heads. That's why they can read maps more easily than women. Women often have to turn a map around in order to know which direction to go, whereas men can do it in their heads. On the other hand, women excel at other spatial tasks such as remembering the location of objects in a random[10] pattern. That's why women

30   are better than men at finding misplaced car keys and eyeglasses.

While it is clear that some differences are rooted in the physiology of the brain, it is equally clear that other differences are not. For example, boys and girls are equal in math ability until about seventh grade. Then girls start to fall behind, perhaps because math teachers encourage boys more. Furthermore,

35   there are many exceptions to these general patterns. Just as some women are good at abstract algebra, some men become skilled poets and public speakers.

Although continuing research will yield further information about gender differences, it will never resolve[11] the battle between the sexes. However, it should help the next time **he** gets lost in the family car while following **her** map-reading

40   directions, and the next time **she** has to look for **his** misplaced car keys.

QUESTIONS ON THE MODEL

1. What is the thesis statement? Double underline it.

2. Does this essay discuss mostly similarities, mostly differences, or both similarities and differences?

3. What is the topic of each body paragraph?

---

[7]**dominant:** more in control; [8]**stutter:** speak with repetition of initial word sounds: b-b-b-boy; [9]**three-dimensional:** having height, width, and depth; [10]**random:** not in any organized sequence; [11]**resolve:** solve

Comparison Structure Words and Phrases

When you want to compare something within a sentence or between two sentences, comparison structure words and phrases are useful. These words and phrases connect the two parts of a comparison of two items, places, persons, and so on. The following table gives a partial list of the most common words and phrases that are used to show similarities.

COMPARISON STRUCTURE WORDS AND PHRASES

| Sentence Connectors | Conjunctions | | | Paired Conjunctions |
	Coordinating	Subordinating	Others	
similarly	and ... (too)	as	just like	both ... and
likewise		just as	the same	not only ... but also
			alike	
also			similar to	
too			the same as	
			the same (... as)	
			equal	
			equally	

Let's study each group of comparison structure words and phrases. (You may want to review the section on transition signals in Unit 5, page 102.)

- Sentence connectors connect two independent clauses. All sentence connectors may be used with a period and a comma between the independent clauses.

  Tokyo is the financial heart of Japan. **Similarly,** New York is the center of banking and finance in the United States.

- Some sentence connectors may also be used with a semicolon and a comma between the independent clauses.

  Tokyo is the financial heart of Japan; **likewise,** New York is the center of banking and finance in the United States.

- The word *also* is generally not used with a semicolon. *Also* may appear in other positions in the second independent clause.

  Tokyo is a major financial center. New York is an important center of banking and finance **also.**
  Tokyo is the financial heart of Japan. New York is **also** an important center of banking and finance.

- The word *too* is usually placed at the end of the second independent clause. It is often used together with the coordinating conjunction *and.*

  Tokyo is a center of style and fashion. New York is, **too.**
  Tokyo is a center of style and fashion, and New York is, **too.**

- The subordinating conjunction *just as* begins a dependent clause.

  Tokyo is crowded and noisy **just as** New York is.
  Tokyo has traffic problems **just as** New York does.

- Notice the difference in usage between *just as* and *just like* in the "Others" list in the chart. *Just as* is a subordinating conjunction and is followed by a subject and a verb. *Just like* is a preposition and is followed by a noun or noun phrase.

  Tokyo is crowded and noisy **just as** New York is.
  Tokyo is crowded and noisy **just like** New York.

- Other comparison structure words and phrases are used to show comparisons within sentences. The part of speech each comparison word or phrase is given in parenthesis.

  Tokyo's traffic is **similar** to New York's. (prepositions)
  The streets in downtown Tokyo and New York City are **alike**. (adjective)
  The subway system in New York City is **the same as** the one in Tokyo. (noun + preposition)
  The shopping areas are **the same**. (noun phrase)
  The exclusive shops in Tokyo display **the same** fashions **as** the exclusive shops in New York. (noun + preposition)
  Tokyo and New York City are **equally** crowded. (adverb)
  Tokyo and New York City have **equal** traffic problems.(adjective)

- Paired conjunctions are always used together. Notice that the word that comes after the second conjunction must be the same part of speech (noun, verb, prepositional phrase, etc.) as the word that comes after the first conjunction. This is an important rule in English and is called the rule of **parallelism.**

  Right: The two cities are both **noisy** (adjective) and **crowded** (adjective).
  Wrong: The two cities are both **busy** (adjective) and **have too many people** (verb phrase).

  Both **New York City** and **Tokyo** have outstanding international restaurants. (nouns)
  Tokyoites and New Yorkers can both **eat** and **drink** in any kind of restaurant. (verbs)
  The two cities have both **positive** and **negative** features. (adjectives)
  Not only **Tokyoites** but also **New Yorkers** dress fashionably. (nouns)
  You can see joggers not only **in Central Park** but also **in Hibuya Park.** (prepositional phrases)

PRACTICE:
Comparison Words

Circle all of the words that show similarities in the model essay on pages 200–201.

PRACTICE:
*Paired
Conjunctions*

Complete the following sentences. Be sure to follow the rule of parallelism.

1. Both in Tokyo and <u>in New York City</u>   the art museums display many famous masterpieces.

2. Both overcrowded subways and _____ are problems in Tokyo and New York City.

3. You can buy designer clothes not only in boutiques but also

   _____ .

4. New Yorkers and Tokyoites not only can see a movie but also

   _____ at any time.

(continued on the next page)

5. In the summer, the weather in Tokyo and in New York is both hot and

_____ .

6. The Ginza and Fifth Avenue shopping districts have both fine jewelers and

_____ .

Write a new sentence comparing the two sentences in each of the following
pairs, using the given comparison structure words. Punctuate correctly.

1. Advertising brings the public information about a product or a service. It is
used to sell an idea or an event. (similarly)

Advertising brings the public information about a product; similarly, it is

used to sell an idea or an event.

2. Advertisements influence a person's choice of food and other daily
necessities. They influence a person's choice of vacation spots and
restaurants. (not only . . . but also)

_____

_____

3. Advertising influences people's spending habits. It raises their standard of
living. (both . . . and)

_____

_____

4. Advertising creates a desire for better clothing. Advertising creates a desire
for a more attractive personal appearance. (not only . . . but also)

_____

_____

5. Newspaper and magazines are largely supported by advertising. Radio and
television are largely supported by advertising. (just as)

_____

_____

6. Newspapers are important advertising media because they reach millions of
readers. Magazines are important advertising media because they reach
millions of readers. (like)

_____

_____

PRACTICE:
Sentence of Comparison

Write sentences of comparison using the given information.

1. The Spanish language/the Italian language/in grammar and vocabulary

   (similar to) _The Spanish language is similar to the_

   Italian language in grammar and vocabulary.

2. Learning to speak English/learning to write English/important

   (both . . . and) _____

   _____

3. School sports are enjoyed/by male students/by female students

   (alike) _____

   _____

4. A high school student who is continuing on to college/a high school student who is not going on to college/graduation requirements.

   (the same . . . as) _____

   _____

5. Private universities/public colleges/good education

   (and . . . too) _____

   _____

6. Books at a private university/books at a public college/cost

   (the same as) _____

   _____

7. Students in private colleges don't just study all the time/students in public colleges participate in sports, clubs, drama, music, and other extra-curricular activities.

   (similarly) _____

   _____

8. Exercising daily keeps a body strong/eating nutritious food/necessary for good health

   (likewise) _____

   _____

Contrast Structure Words and Phrases

Now that you have learned to use comparison structure words and phrases to show how two things are the same, in this section you will learn to use contrast structure words and phrases to show how two things are different. These words and phrases connect the two parts of a contrast between two items, places, persons, and so on. The following table gives a partial list of the most common words and phrases that are used to show differences.

CONTRAST STRUCTURE WORDS AND PHRASES

Sentence Connectors	Conjunctions		Others
	Coordinating	**Subordinating**	
on the other hand	but	although even though	different from unlike
in contrast			
however	yet	while whereas	

Now let's study each group of contrast structure words and phrases.

- Remember that sentence connectors connect two independent clauses. Contrast sentence connectors may be used with either a period and a comma or a semicolon and a comma between the independent clauses:

Men excel at math. **In contrast,** women are better at language.
Men excel at math; **on the other hand,** women are better at language.

- The two coordinating conjunctions in the chart have slightly different uses.
  1. Use *but* when the information in the second clause is in complete contrast to the information in the first clause.

  Men listen primarily with their right ear, **but** women listen with both ears.

  2. Use *yet* when the information in the second clause is unexpected or surprising.

  The language center is in the left side of the brain in both sexes; **yet** women have stronger language skills than men.

NOTE: You can use *but* in place of *yet*.

The language center is in the left side of the brain in both sexes, **but** women have stronger language skills than men.

- Subordinating conjunctions begin a dependent clause. There are differences in meaning and comma use between the two pairs of contrast subordinators in the chart.
  1. Use *although/even though* when the result in the independent clause is an unexpected surprise because of the information given in the dependent clause.

  Even though I took the driving test three times, I couldn't pass it.
  I couldn't pass the driving test **although** I took it three times.

2. Use *while/whereas* when the information in the first clause is in strong contrast (direct opposition) to the information in the second clause.

Some people like to exercise indoors, **while** others prefer to exercise outdoors.
Whereas some people like to exercise indoors, others prefer to exercise outdoors.

Notice that a comma is placed after the independent clause before *while* or *whereas* to show contrast (direct opposition). This is an exception to the usual rule.

- The two other contrast structure words in the "Others" list are prepositions and are used as follows:

Men's spatial abilities are **different from** women's (spatial abilities).
Men are **different from** women in their spatial skills.
Women's spatial abilities are **unlike** men's (spatial abilities).
Unlike men, women use both ears to listen.

PRACTICE:
Contrast Structure Words

A. Circle all of the words that show contrast in the model essay on pages 200–201.

B. Write contrast sentences using the given information. Use a coordinator, a subordinator, and a sentence connector.

1. Jose swims well. Maria swims poorly.

  a. Jose swims well, but Maria swims poorly.

  b. Jose swims well, whereas Maria swims poorly.

  c. Jose swims well; however, Maria swims poorly.

2. Fresh fruit and vegetables taste delicious. Canned fruits and vegetables are tasteless.

  a. _____

  b. _____

  c. _____

3. Eating well and exercising will keep you in good health. Exercising by itself will not.

  a. _____

  b. _____

  c. _____

4. A university has a graduate school. A college usually does not.

  a. _____

  b. _____

  c. _____

(continued on the next page)

5. Mark will go to college on a full scholarship. Carlos will have to work part time.

   a. _____

   b. _____

   c. _____

6. In England, medical care is free. In the United States, people must pay for medical care.

   a. _____

   b. _____

   c. _____

PRACTICE:
Contrast
Sentences

A. Complete the following sentences. Punctuate correctly.

1. I love to go camping, but _my sister doesn't._____

2. Betty has gained ten pounds yet _____

   _____

3. She should exercise although _____

   _____

4. _____

   _____ whereas Susan jogs every day.

5. Climbing mountains is great exercise. On the other hand _____

   _____

6. Living on an island is different from _____

   _____

B. Work with a partner. Take turns saying and writing sentences showing differences between men and women. Use the contrast structure words in parentheses.

1. (on the other hand) _____

   _____

2. (while) _____

   _____

3. (whereas) _____

_____

4. (different from) _____

_____

5. (although) _____

_____

Comparison-Contrast Structure Words

Review the outline you prepared about Alaska and Hawaii. Write a report to your client telling about the two states as a destination. You might begin your report by reminding your client that he or she asked for advice on where to spend his/her vacation and then by writing a few general sentences about Alaska and Hawaii. Follow your outline, which uses block organization for the body of your report. End your report with a recommendation to your client.

With a partner, edit and revise your report. Check your own and your partner's reports, especially for the appropriate use of comparison-contrast structure words.

PART 3 Grammar and Mechanics

Comparisons with Adjectives and Adverbs

> When you are comparing two or more things, adjectives and adverbs of comparison are useful.

You use the **comparative** form of an adjective or adverb to show the differences between two things. You use the **superlative** form to show how one thing differs from two or more things.

Study the examples on the next page, and then complete the chart on page 211.

COMPARATIVE AND SUPERLATIVE FORMS OF ADJECTIVES AND ADVERBS

ONE-SYLLABLE WORDS: *-er than, the . . . -est*		
ADJECTIVES	strict stricter than the strictest	Parents in the United States are **strict.** Parents in Europe are **stricter than** parents in the United States. Parents in Asia are **the strictest** of all.
ADVERBS	fast faster than the fastest	French is spoken **fast.** Italian is spoken **faster than** French. Spanish is spoken **the fastest** of all.
TWO or MORE SYLLABLES: *more/less than, the most/the least*		
ADJECTIVES	challenging more challenging than the most challenging	Algebra is a **challenging** math class. Trigonometry is **more challenging than** algebra. Calculus is **the most challenging** math class in high school.
ADVERBS	casually less casually than the least casually	Elementary school teachers dress **casually** in the United States. High school teachers dress **less casually than** elementary school teachers. University professors dress **the least casually** of all.

WORDS ENDING IN *-y, -le, -er,* and *-ow: -er than, the . . . -est*	
easy, easier than, the easiest gentle, gentler than, the gentlest clever, cleverer than, the cleverest narrow, narrower than, the narrowest	French is **easier than** German. Labrador retrievers are **the gentlest** dogs in the world. She's **cleverer than** her sister. The **narrowest** house in Amsterdam is only ten meters wide.
IRREGULAR FORMS	
good, better than, the best well, better than, the best bad, worse than, the worst little, less than, the least	Which country has **the best** schools? Some students learn **better** by listening **than** by reading. My second-grade teacher was **the worst** teacher I ever had. She had **little** patience with the students.

PRACTICE:
Comparisons with Adjectives and Adverbs

A. With a partner or a small group, complete the chart. If you don't know the meaning of a word, look it up in a dictionary or ask your instructor.

B. Take turns using each word from the chart in a meaningful sentence. You may be able to use some of these words in the essay that you will write at the end of the chapter.

Base Word	Comparative Form	Superlative Form
1. good	better than	the best
2.	stricter than/less strict than	
3.		the most/the least casual
4.	more/less traditional than	
5. rigid		
6.		the most/the least energetic
7. lenient		
8.	more/less formal than	
9.		the worst
10. well-behaved		
11.	more/less close-knit than	
12. respectful		
13.		the most/the least hardworking
14. liberal		
15.	more/less conservative than	
16. harsh		
17. independent		
18.		the most/the least demanding

Comparisons with Nouns

Comparative and **superlative forms** are used not only with adjectives and adverbs but also with nouns.

COMPARISONS WITH NOUNS

Countable Nouns	
more ... than, the most	California has **more** two-year colleges **than** other states. California has **the most** two-year colleges of any state in the United States.
fewer ... than, the fewest	There are **fewer** cars per family in Japan **than** (there are) in the United States. China has **the fewest** cars, but it has **the most** bicycles.

Uncountable Nouns	
more ... than, the most	Children in my country show **more respect** to their parents **than** children in the United States (do). Medical doctors have **the most** respect of any profession in the United States.
less ... than, the least	There is **less** pressure to go to college in public schools **than** (there is) in private schools. Preschool teachers earn **the least** money.

PRACTICE:
Comparisons with Nouns

Complete the following sentences with the correct comparative or superlative form.

CAUTION: Use the correct forms for things that can be counted and things that cannot be counted.

My new apartment has (greater amount) _____more_____
a.
sunlight than my old one. However, it has (smaller number)

_____ rooms. Now I pay $550 per month. I paid
b.
$585 for my last apartment. So, I pay (smaller amount)

_____ rent now. Therefore, I can save (greater
c.
amount) _____ money to buy a new sofa for my
d.
living room. The one I want costs (greater amount)

_____ $700. Right now, I have (smaller amount)
e.
_____ $200 in the bank. However, I should be able
f.
to buy the new sofa in (smaller number) _____
g.
a year.

Expressions of Equality and Inequality

When the two items you are comparing are equal, use *as* + adjective/adverb + *as*. With nouns, use *as much/many* + noun + *as*. To show that things are not equal, make the verb negative.

EXPRESSIONS OF EQUALITY AND INEQUALITY

Adjectives	The fishing in Alaska is **as good as** the fishing in Hawaii.	
	Traveling by train isn't **as convenient as** driving your own car.	
Adverbs	Parents in the United States don't discipline their children **as harshly as** parents in other countries (do).	
	We don't have tests **as frequently as** students in other countries (do).	
Nouns	Countable	Students in my country spend **as many years** in school **as** students in the United States (do).
	Uncountable	Students in my country don't have **as much homework** as students in the United States (do)

PRACTICE:
Expressions of Equality and Inequality

Work with a partner or by yourself. Write sentences to show equality or inequality based on the situation given. Use *as . . . as* or *not as . . . as* in your sentences. There are several possible sentences you could write for each situation.

1. Children in my country help with household chores. Children in the United States also help with housework.

   Children in my country do as much housework as children in the United States do.
   or
   Children in my country do as many household chores as children in the United States do.
   or
   Children in my country help around the house as often as children in the United States do.
   or
   Children in my country are as helpful around the house as children in the United States are.

2. Teachers in my country spend ten hours a day at school. Teachers in the United States spend eight hours a day at school.

   _____

3. Tests are given regularly in my country. Students in the United States are also tested regularly.

   _____

4. There are many excellent universities in my country. There are many excellent universities in the United States.

   _____

(continued on the next page)

5. Books are inexpensive in my country. Books cost a lot of money in the United States.

_____

6. Discipline is harsh in elementary school. Discipline is harsh in high school.

_____

PART 4 The Writing Process

On Your Own!

Now let's complete the writing process you began at the beginning of the unit. Write a well-organized comparison-contrast essay based on Activity 1 on pages 191–192 or Activity 2 on pages 192–193. Follow these steps in order to write a good essay.

STEP 1:
Prewrite to Get Ideas

This is the step you completed at the beginning of the unit.

STEP 2:
Organize the Ideas

Prepare an outline using the block method of organization.

- Rearrange the information from the chart into a block of similarities and a block of differences.
- Decide on the number of paragraphs of comparison and the number of paragraphs of contrast.
- Decide which "block" to put first: similarities or differences.
- Add specific facts, examples, or quotations for each point.
- Write a thesis statement and a concluding sentence.

STEP 3:
Write the Rough Draft

Write ROUGH DRAFT at the top of your paper. Write a rough draft from your outline. Use a variety of comparison and contrast structure words and phrases.

STEP 4:
Edit the Rough Draft

Edit your rough draft. Follow the editing procedure you used in previous units.

EDITING CHECKLIST

Writer's Questions	Peer Editor's Answers and Comments
FORMAT	
1. Is the format correct?	Check the title, indenting, margins, and double spacing.
ORGANIZATION	
2. Does the essay have an introduction, a body, and a conclusion?	How many paragraphs does the essay have? How many paragraphs are in the body?
Introduction **3.** Do the general statements • give background information?	How many general statements are there? Is this a funnel introduction? yes no
• attract the reader's attention?	Does it stimulate your interest in the topic? yes no
4. Does the thesis statement state the topics that will be compared and contrasted?	Copy the thesis statement here:
Body **5.** Does the essay use "block" organization?	Which is discussed first, similarities or differences? How many paragraphs discuss similarities? How many paragraphs discuss differences?
6. Does each body paragraph have • a clearly stated topic sentence with a main (controlling) idea?	Write the main idea for each body paragraph:
• good development with sufficient supporting details?	List one supporting detail from each body paragraph:
• transitions between paragraphs?	List the transitions between each body paragraph:
Conclusion **7.** Does the conclusion • summarize the main points?	Does the conclusion make a judgment or is it neutral? judgment neutral
• give a final comment?	If there is a judgment, is the judgment supported by the facts presented in the essay? yes no
GRAMMAR AND MECHANICS	
8. Are commas used where necessary?	Circle any comma errors. Add missing commas.
9. Are verb tenses used appropriately?	Check each verb for the appropriate tense. Circle any that you have questions about.

SENTENCE STRUCTURE	
10. Do all sentences contain at least one subject and one verb and express a complete thought?	Underline any sentences that you have doubts about.
11. Does the essay contain a variety of sentence types?	What sentence type does this writer use the most often? Circle one: simple compound complex
12. Are comparison and contrast structure words used?	List some comparison and contrast structure words used:

STEP 5:
Write the Second Draft

Write SECOND DRAFT at the top of your paper. Write the second draft of your essay to hand in to your instructor.

STEP 6:
Write the Final Draft

After your instructor returns your paper, write a neat final copy to hand in for final evaluation. Write FINAL DRAFT at the top of your paper.

ADDITIONAL WRITING

For additional practice, compare and contrast any two things such as

Two computer systems (IBM and Apple, for instance)

Two automobiles

Two restaurants/two department stores in your area

Human workers and robots

Public schools and private schools

Growing up in a big city and growing up in the suburbs/in a small town

Appendix A: Correction Symbols

	Meaning	Incorrect	Correct
P.	punctuation	I live, and go to school here. Where do you work.	I live and go to school here. Where do you work?
◯	word missing	I working in a restaurant.	I am working in a restaurant.
Cap.	capitalization	It is located at main and baker streets in the City.	It is located at Main and Baker Streets in the city.
v.t.	verb tense	I never work as a cashier until I get a job there.	I had never worked as a cashier until I got a job there.
agr.	subject-verb agreement	The manager work hard. There is five employees.	The manager works hard. There are five employees.
⌣	make one word or sentence	Every one works hard. We work together. So we have become friends.	Everyone works hard. We work together, so we have become friends.
sp.	spelling	The maneger is a woman.	The manager is a woman.
pl.	plural	She treats her employees like slave.	She treats her employees like slaves.
⊘	unnecessary word	My boss she watches everyone all the time.	My boss watches everyone all the time.
w.f.	wrong word form	Her voice is irritated.	Her voice is irritating.
w.w.	wrong word	The food is delicious. Besides, the restaurant is always crowded.	The food is delicious. Therefore, the restaurant is always crowded.
ref.	pronoun reference error	The restaurant's specialty is fish. They are always fresh. The food is delicious. Therefore, it is always crowded.	The restaurant's specialty is fish. It is always fresh. The food is delicious. Therefore, the restaurant is always crowded.

Symbol	Meaning	Example	Correction
∽	wrong word order	Friday always is our busiest night.	Friday is always our busiest night.
RO OR CS	run-on OR comma splice (incorrectly joined independent clauses)	Lily was fired she is upset. (RO) / Lily was fired, she is upset. (CS)	Lily was fired, so she is upset. Lily was fired; therefore, she is upset. Because Lily was fired, she is upset. Lily is upset because she was fired.
FRAG	fragment (incomplete sentence)	She was fired. Because she was always late.	She was fired because she was always late.
Ⓣ	add a transition	She was also careless. She frequently spilled coffee on the table.	She was also careless. For example, she frequently spilled coffee on the table.
S.	subject	Is open from 6:00 PM until the last customer leaves.	The restaurant is open from 6:00 PM until the last customer leaves.
V.	verb	The employees on time and work hard.	The employees are on time and work hard.
prep.	preposition	We start serving dinner 6:00 PM.	We start serving dinner at 6:00 PM.
conj.	conjunction	The garlic shrimp, fried clams, broiled lobster are the most popular dishes.	The garlic shrimp, fried clams, and broiled lobster are the most popular dishes.
art.	article	Diners expect glass of water when they first sit down at table.	Diners expect a glass of water when they first sit down at the table.
¶	Symbol for a paragraph		

Appendix B: Kinds of Sentences

SIMPLE SENTENCES = one independent clause:

> subject + verb
> subject + verb + complement

Spring has arrived!
The flowers are blooming.
The sun is shining brightly.
People are walking and jogging in the park.

COMPOUND SENTENCES = two independent clauses

The sun is shining, and there are no clouds in the sky.
The sun is shining; there are no clouds in the sky.
The sun is shining; furthermore, there are no clouds in the sky.

COMPLEX SENTENCES = one independent clause + one (or more) dependent clauses

Rollerblading is great fun when you skate with a group of people.
Although rollerblading with the group is fun, you have to skate fast to keep up.
Alex broke his arm because he fell when he skated too fast.

Appendix C: Connectors

COORDINATING CONJUNCTIONS

for	and	nor	but	or	yet	so

PAIRED CONJUNCTIONS

both . . . and

not only . . . but also
neither . . . nor

SUBORDINATING CONJUNCTIONS

ADVERB CLAUSES

Time
after
as soon as
before
since
until
when
whenever
while

Place
where
wherever

Reason
as
because
since

Purpose
in order that
so that

Condition
as if
even if
if
unless

Comparison
just as

Contrast
although
even though
whereas
while

ADJECTIVE CLAUSES

Person
that
who
whom
whose

Thing
that
which
whose

Place
where

Time
when

SENTENCE CONNECTORS and PREPOSITIONS

Additional Idea
also
besides
finally
furthermore
in addition
moreover

(Prepositions)
besides . . .
in addition to . . .

**Opposite Idea /
Contrast**
however
in contrast
on the other hand

(Prepositions)
despite . . .
in spite of . . .
unlike . . .

**Similarity /
Comparison**
also
likewise
similarly

(Prepositions)
similar to . . .
like . . .

Effect or Result
as a result
consequently
therefore
thus

Example
for example
for instance

(Like a preposition)
. . . such as . . .

Choice or Alternative
otherwise

OTHER TRANSITION EXPRESSIONS

Opinions
According to _____ , . . .
In my opinion, . . .
In my view, . . .
I think / believe / feel (that) . . .

Conclusions
All in all, . . .
For these reasons, . . .
In brief, . . .
Indeed, . . .
In other words, . . .
In short, . . .
In the end, . . .

Time Order
First, . . .
First of all, . . .
Second, . . .
Next, . . .
After that, . . .
Afterward, . . .
Later, . . .
Finally, . . .
Meanwhile, . . .
Then . . .
Now . . .
At the beginning of the . . . ,
Before the . . . ,
After the . . . ,
During the . . . ,
On the day of the . . . ,

Spatial Order
above the
across from the
around the outside of the
at the top of the
below the
behind the
beside the
between the
close to the
in the
in (the) back (of) the
in (the) front (of) the
in the center (of the)
inside (of) the
near the
next to the
on one side of the
on the other side of the
on the left (right)
opposite the
to the left (right) of the
under the

Order of Importance
The first and most important
reason is. . .
The last and most important
reason is . . .

Appendix D: Summary of Punctuation Rules

END-OF-SENTENCE PUNCTUATION

Put a period at the end of a statement or command.

The flowers are beautiful in the spring.
Water the flowers today.

Put a question mark at the end of a question.

Why are your roses dying?

Use an exclamation point to show strong feeling.

Well, I'm not a gardener!

COMMAS ARE USED

To separate items in a series.

I'm taking Spanish, English, physics, and economics.
The teacher will read your essay, make comments on it, and return it to you.

To separate the day of the month from the year, and after the year.

Americans declared their independence from England on July 4, 1776, in Philadelphia.

NOTE: If no day is given, no commas are necessary.

Americans declared their independence from England in July 1776 in Philadelphia.

To separate the parts of an address in a sentence.

My address is 401 West 63rd Street, Apt. 13, New York, New York.

To separate the street name from the apartment number and the city from the state in a postal address.

401 West 63rd Street, Apt. 13
New York, NY 10017

Before a coordinating conjunction in a compound sentence.

We don't need to bring umbrellas, for the sun is shining brightly.

After a sentence connector in a compound sentence.

The sun is shining brightly; therefore, we don't need to bring umbrellas.

After a dependent adverbial clause that is followed by an independent clause in a complex sentence.

Because the sun is shining brightly, we don't need to bring umbrellas.

Before (and after) nonrestrictive adjective clauses.

The Napa Valley, which is a famous wine-growing region in Northern California, is about 100 miles north of San Francisco.

Before (and after) nonrestrictive appositives.

The Napa Valley, a famous wine-growing region in Northern California, is about 100 miles north of San Francisco.

After most transition expressions at the beginning of a sentence.

Finally, we arrived at our hotel.
However, our rooms were not ready.
After an hour, we left to find a place to eat.
Across the street, we found a small cafe.

SEMICOLONS ARE USED

Between independent clauses that are not connected by a coordinating conjunction in a compound sentence.

My battery is dead; my car won't start.
My battery is dead; therefore, my car won't start.

QUOTATION MARKS ARE USED

Around the words of a direct quotation.

She said, "I'll miss you."
"I'll write you every day," she promised.
"I'll think about you every day," she continued, "and I'll dream about you every night."

Index